THE BIGGEST *Lies*

A Woman's Journey through the Wilderness

D. A. COFFER

ISBN 978-1-0980-7488-3 (paperback)
ISBN 978-1-0980-7489-0 (digital)

Copyright © 2021 by D. A. Coffer

All rights reserved. No part of this publication may be reproduced, distributed, or transmitted in any form or by any means, including photocopying, recording, or other electronic or mechanical methods without the prior written permission of the publisher. For permission requests, solicit the publisher via the address below.

Christian Faith Publishing, Inc.
832 Park Avenue
Meadville, PA 16335
www.christianfaithpublishing.com

Unless otherwise noted, all scripture references are taken from the King James Version (KJV).

Printed in the United States of America

For Hannah

Contents

Preface 7
Acknowledgments 9
Prologue: My Backstory 11
Introduction 13

Part 1: The Lies
Lie #1: I Can Do What I Want 19
Lie #2: Being Lukewarm Is Enough 27
Lie #3: Never Good Enough 33
Lie #4: I Can Have the Best of Both Worlds 39
Lie #5: It's Too Late for Me 45
Lie #6: God's Not Really All That Interested in Me 52
Lie #7: You Should Just Believe in Yourself 59
Lie #8: I Can't Forgive That Person 65

Part 2: God's Truths
Truth # 1: Eternity Is a Choice 73
Truth # 2: His Grace Is Sufficient 78
Truth # 3: God Wants to Place Your Feet on Solid Ground 89
Truth # 4: The Blessings of God Are Real 95
Truth # 5: He Will Never Leave You or Forsake You 101
Truth # 6: He Never Fails Us 108
Truth # 7: You Can Do All Things through Christ 112
Truth # 8: We Are All Missionaries 116

The Conclusion of the Matter: Give Me Oil in My Lamp 121
Epilogue: Your Greatest Enemy Is Fear 125

PREFACE

The *joy* of the Lord *is* my strength.

My whole life, the devil has worked at tearing down my self-confidence, reducing me to a self-conscious, damaged woman who never believed that she could be what God told her He created her to be. Every time I thought I was rising, getting more confident, I would find myself slammed back down to the ground. I never really believed that I could do the things that God was revealing that He wanted me to do, that I would ever be confident enough to share my story with others. But I finally stopped listening to the father of lies and turned my eyes and my faith to the Father of Light. This is my story.

Acknowledgments

Father, thank You for not allowing the lowest points of my life to limit my potential. Thank You for giving divine purpose to someone as imperfect as me. I praise You for Your amazing power that carries me in moments of weakness. I know that no matter where I started, You will take me where You want me to go. Thank You, Jesus, for showing me that incredible things begin in humble places.

Thank you to my wonderful husband, Gregg, and my daughters, Hannah, Morgan, and Maverick, for standing beside me throughout this arduous journey. For it has, indeed, been just that—a journey! Especially Maverick, who tirelessly let me read and reread drafts of each chapter to her, never complaining, always listening to the will of the Spirit to help guide my writing. I couldn't have finished my story without you!

Thank you to my colleagues and friends who have been so encouraging and supportive as I found (and fought) my way through the chapters, especially when I thought I couldn't keep writing, especially Cathy, Afton, and Karen, who let me share glimpses of my past with you, never judging, always loving me in spite of my flaws, and giving the very best kind of advice!

A very special shout out to Pastor Stacy, who wasn't afraid to "get me told" on an occasion or two, keeping my feet out of the flames. You always told me you'd rather get to heaven and find out you had more Jesus than you needed than to miss heaven because you didn't have enough! I keep that advice close to me. And thank you, Sister Jennifer, for always believing I'd land on my feet!

And finally, a very heartfelt thank you to Valerie. Girl, words are not enough. You saved my life!

PROLOGUE

My Backstory

> It's about sharing life,
> and giving our own away.
> It's about serving God.
> It's about saving grace.
> —Point of Grace, "Saving Grace"

As I begin writing this, I can honestly say I have no idea where God is taking me. He gave me the chapter titles and the unction. He asked me to be obedient. I ran from it. I procrastinated. I tried to meld His story into mine. He overwhelmed me with heaviness of heart and took me again and again to the book of Romans.

> I beseech you therefore, brethren, by the mercies of God, that ye present your bodies a living sacrifice, holy, acceptable unto God, which is your reasonable service. And be not conformed to this world: but be ye transformed by the renewing of your mind, that ye may prove what is that good, and acceptable, and perfect, will of God. (Romans 12:1–2)

I had to stop and ponder that Word for a bit and ask myself a few questions. I asked God, "How do I present myself as a living sacrifice?" His response was by submitting myself and surrendering to His will for my life. I thought I had done that, but then I realized if I had, the book would have already been written, as He put it in my heart over a year ago. My next question was "How do I let God transform me and renew my mind?" His answer was through daily dependence on Him for direction in *all* my decisions. This includes my decisions on how to spend my time, which I obviously was not relying on Him for, or once again, the book would have been written.

Finally, I asked, "How do I prove the will of God, His purpose for my life?" His answer was by being obedient to His call, which allows Him to bless me through that obedience. I borrowed the following from the commentary in my study Bible: "When we seek to discern the will of God, we must also commit to doing it." Therefore, obedience brings God's blessings because His will is for our good.

So the short answer to all my questions related to these two verses was to stop what I was doing and get started on the book He wanted me to write. So here it is. I pray as I work through the chapters that I will be led by the Spirit to write what God wants His children to know, that my own ideas and analysis will not overpower His divine leading, and that what comes out of this is truly an inspired work that will bring God glory and help others to find their way to a greater relationship with Him. May God lead me through the pages, pour His Spirit out over me, and work through my hands and my mind to accomplish that good and perfect purpose He has placed in my life. In Jesus's name, amen.

Introduction

We spend so much time trying to prove to the world how good we are that we don't allow them to see just how much, to what great depth, God has rescued us and transformed us. Saying that I'm a Christian (with where I am now) doesn't show anyone else how to escape their darkness. Only by opening my mouth, becoming transparent, and allowing others to see the dark place I came from can I truly show the light of Jesus to the lost. They must first see just how lost I was, and just how dark the darkness was, to fully understand or comprehend just how bright the light of the Savior is.

A person who has never been a slave to the lust of their body can't relate to someone held captive by it. A person who has never had an abortion can't truly empathize with the person who is held captive by the guilt that comes with that decision. Those who are running from God are doing so because the guilt is so strong. But all that guilt and condemnation comes from the devil. Conviction and redemption through repentance comes from God. People who turn away from God in the midst of their sin are running from the very one Who holds the keys, the cure, everything they need. The devil is standing there in front of them, blocking their path, or running beside them, taunting them, whispering in their ear that God could never love them. He's telling them that if God really cared about them, He would never have let them be in this situation to begin with. How could He love them? Why would He even care?

If any of that sounds familiar to you, I urge you to keep reading. I want to tell you upfront that this book is not meant to judge anyone. As Paul wrote, we are all sinners, and I am the chiefest. If you were to list every sin that I have ever committed in my life, the list would be endless. I could never begin to condemn anyone for any sin that they've ever committed. I have done things in my life that I thought I could never talk to anyone about. I ran from God for *so* long.

See, I was the person who thought I had done too much. I was that person who heard the devil whispering in my ear that God could never love me again. I was the one who heard the words, "How could God possibly love you if He let you get to this?" I listened to that broken record for so long during my late teens and into my twenties. I believed the lies for over a decade. But I'm here to tell you that if any of what I said resonates with you, you have fallen victim to the greatest lie the devil tells the sinner.

He tries to tell you that you are weak. He tries to convince you that your life serves no purpose greater than yourself. He tries to tell you that you are nothing. But I'm here to tell you that you are so much more. If you could see yourself the way God sees your soul, you would begin to understand just how beautiful you truly are. You are God's greatest creation. In the book of Genesis, the Word tells us that God created man in His own image. We could've been made into anything. We could've been a lion or a tiger or a bear or a grasshopper. But we are man and woman, created in the image of the Creator of the entire universe.

God would've never created us in His image if our lives didn't serve a purpose. We are the flesh of all the goodness that exists from God. We are His children, and we are here on this earth to learn to be adults. Not adults like the world sees, not by their standard, but by God's standard. When we are saved, we become like children in God's eyes, and He expects us to grow and learn. But in order to learn, we have to experience life. We will make choices, some good, some bad. But it's not so much the choices as it is what we learn from them that matters.

When we make good choices, we please God and we become more like Him. When we make bad choices, just as our own children do in the world, we have to be rebuked and chastised. But even as we chastise our own children for wrongdoing, we never stop loving them. And we rebuke them, not because we don't love them, but because we love them so much that we want them to be okay, we want them to be successful, want them to be safe. And that's why God rebukes and chastises us, His children, to teach us to be wiser, more successful, and safe.

But the devil would have us believe that the rebuking and chastisement is God's way of telling us that we are not good enough. The devil would have us believe that we so disappoint God that He turns His back on us, that He wipes His hands of us, that He has no more use for us. But could you see doing that to your own children when they make mistakes? Could you see yourself telling your own son or daughter that because of something they've done, that you no longer love them or want to be their parent? That's ridiculous. And in the same way—actually in an even greater, more perfect way—God loves us no matter what. But to keep the relationship strong, we have to realize our mistakes. We have to listen to Him when He corrects us and chastises us, and we have to repent of the sins that we have committed. Then we have to turn from our sins and begin to experience a new life in Christ.

Sure, we're still going to make mistakes along the way. Mistakes define us. They teach us and help mold who we are. Now I'm not saying that we should purposely make mistakes. Because for every mistake, there are ramifications or consequences. The sins that I have committed have come with pain. Sometimes it's been a pain that seemed so unbearable that I just wanted to quit, to give up. But it was when I threw myself at the feet of a loving and merciful Savior that I found forgiveness, I found restoration, and I found the strength to stand back up and to continue moving forward in my life. And I've learned not to make those same mistakes again.

I've come to realize that all the mistakes that I have made and all the pain that I have experienced have made me who I am. It's made me more loving, more compassionate, less focused on self, and more focused on caring about others. I know if I can *share* some of the pain of the mistakes I've made, and I can share how God, through His mercy and love, picked me back up and set my feet on solid ground, if I can help one person come back to a loving relationship with

Christ, one full of mercy and grace, not condemnation and guilt, then it's worth every word that I have put on paper. It's worth every part of this difficult journey of baring my soul.

God desires that no one should miss out on an eternity in heaven. He beckons all to come to Him. *All.* Not just the perfect, because, in truth, there are no perfect people. But from the worst sinner to the person with the best of intentions, God wants all of us to be saved. We are all sinners in need of a Savior. All of us. And God wants all of us to have a relationship with Him for eternity.

So now that we know this truth, let's go back and examine some of the lies. The Bible tells us that the devil is the "father of lies," the grandmaster, if you will, of twisting and manipulating our perception and experiences to rob us of our joy and, if possible, even our eternity. He wants us to be like an anchorless ship, tossed to and fro on the ocean of despair, crippled by our fears and failures, unable to feel God's presence or fulfill His purpose for our lives. But when we realize how craftily the devil weaves his lies into the fabric of our lives and learn how to stand against him through the power of the Word, that's when his schemes begin to reveal themselves and we are able to stand in victory with our Lord and Savior, Jesus Christ.

My hope, my prayer, is that in sharing with you some of the biggest trials and temptations I have faced, as well as my failures and (*praise God*) my subsequent victories, I can help you to navigate through some of the biggest pillars of deception the devil has set up against us. Though my stories are personal, the lies that led me to those experiences are universal. So let us begin our journey together as we examine some of the biggest *lies* ever told and the *truths* that can set us free.

PART 1

The Lies

LIE #1

I Can Do What I Want

The following is an excerpt from my journal, dated August 11, 2011. This was written the day after I committed adultery. Yes, I said it. One of the greatest sins in my mind a Christian woman can commit, because it's completely about self and absolutely in defiance of God. But I think as you read my journal entry, you will begin to see how the devil lies to us and how easily we can be deceived when we are carried away by our own evil lusts.

> Today I found myself, after searching all these years. I can still be beautiful and sexy at 40 *[self]*. I love cats. I love sunlight, and I am happiest in a room filled with it. I don't need food for comfort, working out makes me feel good all over. I miss watching football. I love kids and teaching, love life, and love Jesus. I'm not perfect, and I've made a lot of choices that I have had to pay for *[I hadn't, really, not in the judgment of God kind of way]*. But, I have a Father in heaven who loves me *[there's one truth]* and wants me to be happy *[see the counterfeit?]*, who heard my sincere *[selfish, self-absorbed, deceived]* crying of my heart, and is allowing me to pursue my dreams *[allowing, yes; blessing, no]*, so long as I

follow Him *[which I obviously was NOT doing]*. The prison door has opened *[or did it just close?]*, the shackles are being loosed *[tightened]*, and it's about time for me to step out into the sun *[hellfire and damnation]*.

I have to stop here. This passage breaks my heart. Do you realize I mentioned "self" twenty-three times (*I*, *me*, *my*, etc.) and only mentioned God or referenced Him four times? There's the problem! God, I am so sorry that I let myself be so deceived. How could I profess to love You and follow You when every line in that entry is about *self*? As I was typing it, God was speaking to me and revealing what I couldn't see then, all the lies and deception taking place as I selfishly followed my own heart and my own carnal, fleshly desires. I thought I would go back and delete those phrases as I described them, but God is telling me to leave them there, so I am leaving them in brackets and italics.

I imagine you are lost at this point, wondering what this has to do with adultery, or perhaps it is clear to you already. This is the hard part for me because it requires me to share things that are deeply personal.

At the time I had written the journal entry, I was at a major crossroads in my life, and not in a good way. It could have been good if I had fallen on my knees, asked God to forgive me right then and there, and turned back to serving Him. But I didn't. I followed the lie instead. I had committed adultery. I was leaving a thirteen-year relationship (eleven years of marriage) for an old flame from fifteen years earlier. The lie was so crafty, so believable. That's the part God wants you to understand. It's not about me falling into the sin of adultery. We all face various temptations. It's more about how the devil manipulates the truth into lies, and how easily we can be deceived if we are not on our guard. Even when we think we are running strong, we can still trip and fall. Let me explain.

Imagine this for a moment. You've been unhappy in your marriage for a couple of years. You don't feel like your needs are being met, you're having issues with your husband, he isn't doing what you want him to do, and you hit kind of a midlife crisis moment when you feel like life is passing you by. In a moment of weakness, you cry out to God (verbally, where the devil can hear it) that you want out. God hears your anguish, honors your honesty, and begins to work things out for you. You can't see everything He is doing but, rest assured, He is responding. Faith would say be patient and wait on God.

> Therefore, being justified by faith, we have peace with God through our Lord Jesus Christ: By whom also we have access by faith into this grace wherein we stand, and rejoice in hope of the glory of God. And not only so, but we glory in tribulations also: knowing that tribulation worketh patience; And patience, experience; and experience, hope: And hope maketh not ashamed; because the love of God is shed abroad in our hearts by the Holy Ghost which is given unto us. (Romans 5:1–5)

And if I could have just stayed focused on the Word and on God's promises, everything would have turned out all right. I even testified about it, about how less than a week after I prayed to God about wanting out, He turned things around for us financially, with a *huge* blessing that would have led to so much good in my marriage. That blessing would have, in time, opened the door for the other things to fall in line. It wasn't about the money—ever! It was about God hearing me and acknowledging my heartache. The financial turnaround was just a sign, a confirmation that God heard my cry, and was working things out for us, for my marriage, for my worries, for my discontent—all of it.

How could I have been so blind? I could see it at that moment in June. I could see God moving in a magnificent way. And I was giving Him glory! But I had forgotten something, and this is the part God wants you to know and understand. At the same time that He was working things out for a blessing, the devil was devising a plan, an evil, crafty, deceptive plan, that he was sure I would fall for. Because, you see, when I cried out to God that night, I did it audibly, and God was not the only one listening. The Bible tells us that the devil roams to and fro, looking for who He can deceive. And that night, when I prayed that prayer, the devil had just the foothold he needed. And he set his plan into action. Let me show you...

All these things happened in June and July. Our finances were rearranged supernaturally, to where we had more than enough money to pay bills and live comfortably, which would allow each of us to pursue our dreams and passions. That same month, I read *The Notebook* and watched the movie, loving both. The theme of unrequited love echoed in my hurting heart. Just a few short weeks later, my stepfather passed away, leaving my mom alone and fragile, which started many conversations about what could have been with my real dad.

This led to an outing in which I had lunch with my mom and sister. During our meal, I brought up some of my marital discontents, and we began talking about past loves, especially the "ones that got away." My mom talked about my dad and her regrets; my sister talked about an ex-husband and her regrets; and somehow the name of one of my ex-boyfriends came up, one from fifteen years before. We looked him up on Facebook and discovered he looked amazing after all those years, and I realized I was still very much attracted to him (flesh again). As the days passed, I began lusting after him and the physical relationship we had enjoyed all those years ago (flesh again times one hundred).

The *very* next morning, I received a Facebook message from the ex-boyfriend I had just been talking about, telling me he still thought about me, that I was "forever" in his heart, and ending with "I love you." Mind blown, I replied with the message, "Me too." And thus began a dialogue between us about the past. Around the same time, I planned a trip to South Dakota to visit my dad. My mom decided she wanted to go with me so she could see an old friend and ultimately to see if the old flame was still alive. My husband decided he was not going to make the trip with us but chose instead to take his own minivacation.

Just before I left on the trip, in my frustration with everything that was happening, including the fact that he didn't want to go, I gave my husband an ultimatum that things needed to change or we were headed for a divorce. Then I spent a solid week away from him, back in my childhood city, listening to my mom and dad talk about the past, while spending every night on the phone talking with my ex-boyfriend about our past and how unhappy each of us was in our current relationships. Yes, the warning signs were already there, but I was too wrapped up in my emotions to see beyond my flesh.

I came home from the trip, determined things would change or I was giving up. I was met with sadness and hopelessness from a man who thought he had given me everything I wanted, who didn't know how to give me anything else. A month passed of continued unhappiness at home, as long, private conversations with my ex moved from talking about the past to dreaming of a future together. And then I made the decision to take another road trip, this time to do what my mom had done and get face-to-face with my memories of the past.

The deception didn't stop there. Once the devil had a foothold, he began whispering to me…constantly. The stage was set; the net was readied. I had stopped listening to God and started believing everything the devil was telling me. I was making trips to the altar, asking for prayer, begging God to take away the temptation. That was the problem. It was time for me to be happy. It was time for me to do what I wanted. And I had the foolishness to believe that all these "coincidences" had come together by God's design rather than realizing it was the devil. When I prayed, I was telling God what to do. I was asking Him to bend to *my* will. I was demanding that He act on my behalf, rather than me following the directions He gives us in His Word.

He spoke to me, loudly, and I heard the words He said, but I wasn't listening. He spoke, very plainly, two things. The first was that He was working things out according to His will, and that I might not understand it, but it was going to turn out for my good. The other was that if I continued to follow my own desire, it was going to bring pain, and a lot of it. I was so foolish. I took what He was telling me, and I let the devil twist it around to meet my own desires and support my decisions instead of falling on my knees and repenting. When you do that, you have to remember, the flesh is weak.

So now that you can see the lie, and it seemed like the devil had won the battle, how does God get the glory in the end? It is only now, more than five years later, that I finally get it. Through all that temptation, I kept praying for God to take the temptation out of my way. I confessed that I wasn't strong enough to handle it, and I blamed God for not taking it away from me. I used that as an excuse to justify my actions, to make mistakes and rebel against the Word and my marriage. It is now that I realize that, rather than praying for God to take the temptation away, I *should* have been praying for Him to give me strength to endure the temptation. I *should* have been praying for courage and wisdom so that I could fight against the wiles of the devil and come out on the other side of the trial victorious. Instead, I kept praying for it to go away, while simultaneously making emotional deposits into the relationship.

When Jesus was in the wilderness being tempted by the devil, and the devil started tempting Him during His weakest physical moment, that was when the strength of God was revealed. Jesus didn't ask God to take the devil out of the way. He said He did not live by bread alone but by every word that proceeds out of the mouth of God. He used the Word to stand against temptations. My mistake was that instead of praying for God to take the temptation away, I should have used the Word to stand on my faith and my beliefs to resist the devil and the temptation, which I clearly recognized was wrong (or I wouldn't have been praying against it). *Then* the devil would've had to flee, and *I* would've come out on the other side victorious, having made the right decisions.

I cannot go back, but I can take the lesson forward with me into future moments of temptation. And now the minute I see trouble brewing in my relationship with my current husband, I'm on my knees praying for strength, praying for God's blessing on our relationship, and praying for wisdom to hear God's voice to guide me.

> Ye therefore, beloved, seeing ye know these things before, beware lest ye also, being led away with the error of the wicked, fall from your own stedfastness. (2 Peter 3:17)

*****

So now it's your turn. Think about a time in your life when you felt tempted.

- How did you handle the temptation?

- If you feel you were victorious, what passages from the Word of God gave you the most strength and direction?

- If you feel like you "fell" into the temptation, what warning signs were there that you either didn't see or didn't want to see? What were the consequences?

- How did God bring you through the temptation or restore you (bring you to repentance) after you "fell"?

- What lessons did you learn that could help others facing similar battles?

- If you are in the midst of a battle at this very moment, what steps can you take to get you back in alignment (or keep you in alignment) with God's will and His Word?

- Use the "Quiet Reflections" space on the next page to record your responses and any additional thoughts you have after reading this chapter.

Quiet Reflections

LIE #2

Being Lukewarm Is Enough

God is as real in your life as you want Him to be. And honestly, He's real even when you don't know how real He needs to be.

> Whither shall I go from thy spirit? or whither shall I flee from thy presence? If I ascend up into heaven, thou art there: if I make my bed in hell, behold, thou art there. If I take the wings of the morning, and dwell in the uttermost parts of the sea; Even there shall thy hand lead me, and thy right hand shall hold me. (Psalms 139:7–10)

I get it. Life gets busy. Work, family, friends…responsibilities creep up continuously, and before you know it, your whole day has been spent, and you've left out the most important person in your life. It's not that you forgot He was there or stopped believing in Him. You just did what we all end up doing from time to time. You took your relationship with the Almighty for granted. Sound familiar? It's something I'd be willing to bet we've all been guilty of at some time(s) in our lives. But this message isn't about beating yourself up over a failed relationship. It's about recognizing where you are in that relationship and how much effort you are putting into it yourself. It's about how much you are missing out on by not investing time daily. And how much there is to lose. Let me explain in another way.

If a person is interested in transforming his or her body, going from fluffy and out of shape to athletic and energetic, there's only one way to accomplish that. You have to start exercising. Now, how often you exercise and how long (or how intensely) affects how quickly you see improvements. So if you exercise regularly, over time you will indeed achieve a healthier, leaner physique. Now, it might take you longer than someone else, or your outcome might look different from someone else's, but that's a whole other message (I may circle back later). The point is, you will only get out of your desire to get in shape what you put into it and how often you put into it. Additionally, once you've reached a fitness goal, if you don't continue to work at it regularly, you will find that your progress starts sliding backward and you can end up worse off than when you started.

> When the unclean spirit is gone out of a man, he walketh through dry places, seeking rest, and findeth none. Then he saith, I will return into my house from whence I came out; and when he is come, he findeth it empty, swept, and garnished. Then goeth he, and taketh with himself seven other spirits more wicked than himself, and they enter in and dwell there: and the last state of that man is worse than the first. (Matthew 12:43–45)

Here's my point. Our relationship with the Almighty is the same way. If we want to grow in our relationship with God, we have to invest time and effort regularly and not be content to reach a certain level and then stop there. And just as our muscles and ligaments are ever ready to work for us, God is ever ready to go to work in our lives. But God is a gentleman. He doesn't impose Himself on us. If we want more of Him, He's there waiting to flood our lives with abundant blessings and joy unspeakable. But if we start getting lazy and taking that relationship for granted, He allows us the option to let our relationship grow lukewarm, not because He wants that but because, too often, unconsciously, it's what we want.

Here is where the lie comes in. We rationalize our decision to take a step back, slow things down, and just stick to the status quo. *God, this is all too much. I'm not ready to put myself out there like that. I just want to worship You privately and not draw too much attention to myself. Besides, I don't have the time to engage at that level. I'm just too busy…* Be honest, have you ever subconsciously thought that? I'm certainly not trying to call anyone out here. These are thoughts that have gone through my own mind every time I have started backpedaling in my faith. And, sure enough, any time I stop stoking the fire of obedience to Christ, the flame begins to dwindle. Not His flame for me (that is eternal), but rather, the zeal and determination for being faithful and obedient above all else—yeah, that flame begins to quietly die down. And the devil secretly pats me on the shoulder and says, "Atta girl. You're doing fine. No need to get all crazy." And I believe him, not even realizing who's whispering in my ear.

"Give me oil in my lamp, keep me burning. Give me oil in my lamp, I pray…"

Woe to me if I ever let it go completely out! I'm reminded of the parable of the ten virgins. Know it? The story goes that ten virgins were waiting for the master to arrive, but as he tarried and the night grew long, five of the lamps began running out of oil. And those five virgins had to leave the watch party and go searching for oil. While they were gone, the master returned, and the five virgins who had brought plenty of oil were taken into the marriage supper. The other five returned with new oil, but the master said basically that it was too late, he didn't know who they were, and they couldn't come in to dine.

Now let's put that in relational terms. If we keep working on our relationship with Jesus, spending time daily building up the flame, when Jesus returns, we will be invited into the wedding supper of the lamb (by way of the grave or the Rapture). And hopefully we will hear our Lord say, "Well done, my good and faithful servant."

But what if we let that fire we have for Jesus burn out? It's not that we stopped believing He is the Son of God and the Savior of the world, we've just grown cold, gotten weary of following the "keeper of the stars," and let life and all its busyness choke out the flame that once burned so strongly. What then? Jesus has a very real (and scary) answer for us, and it's found not only in the parable of the ten virgins (as well as other parables) but is stated point-blank in the book of Revelation.

> I know thy works, that thou art neither cold nor hot: I would thou wert cold or hot. So then because thou art lukewarm, and neither cold nor hot, I will spue thee out of my mouth. (Revelation 3:15–16)

That's pretty clear. And if that's not enough, back up a few verses.

> I know thy works, that thou hast a name that thou livest, and art dead. Be watchful, and strengthen the things which remain, that are ready to die: for I have not found thy works perfect before God. Remember therefore how thou hast received and heard, and hold fast, and repent. If therefore thou shalt not watch, I will come on thee as a thief, and thou shalt not know what hour I will come upon thee. (Revelation 3:1–3)

Remember that Jesus wasn't talking to nonbelievers. These were written as warnings to the seven churches—in other words, to believers; that's us—as a warning to not let our flame burn out. My friend, look around you. The earth is growing weary of the sin that is burdening her. God's creation is crying out for the return of its King. Our Lord and Savior Jesus Christ is returning soon. How will He find you? How will He find me? Will our lamps be full of oil? Will our flame be burning brightly? Or will we find ourselves on the outside looking in, wishing we had stoked the fires of our relationship with God while we waited for Christ's return? And while we're on the subject of burning brightly, I want to circle back to a comment

I made earlier. Remember how I said that when you begin working out, your physical progress won't look exactly like someone else's? This is true of your spiritual journey as well. As you draw closer to God, don't try to compare your relationship with God to someone else's journey. We each have our own cross to bear and our own path to walk. I encourage you to lean into your relationship with Jesus and work out your own salvation. Don't gauge the temperature of your flame (your zeal for God) by someone else's fire. Instead, measure it by what you read in the Word and by what God reveals to you as you seek Him through Bible study, worship, and pray.

*****

Now it's your turn. I said in the beginning of this passage that God is as real to us as we want Him to be.

- How real is He to you?

- Do you talk to Him every day?

- Do you take time to worship Him and learn more about Him every day? Or do you take your relationship for granted, expecting Him to do all the work?

- God did everything for us. He sacrificed His Son so that we can have a relationship with Him for eternity. But what are we doing on our end?

- Do you know Him? Do you want to know Him better?

- What is God speaking to you? Record your thoughts on the next page.

Quiet Reflections

LIE #3

Never Good Enough

It doesn't matter how hard I try. I always mess up. It's impossible to live the life of a Christian! I could never be that perfect! Have you ever said those things to yourself? Or something similar? If so, you have experienced another attack (and lie) from the devil. He deceives you by yet another half-truth that he has manipulated to keep you from following Jesus.

> As it is written, there is none righteous, no, not one... (Romans 3:10)
>
> Christianity is not about earning righteousness, it's about receiving the righteousness of Jesus "by faith." It's not about who we are, it's about who He is. (25-Day Advent Devotional)

Jesus became sin for all of us, for everything we ever did, for everything we will ever do wrong...forever! One sacrifice to cover all the sins of all time. And when we accept Jesus as our Lord and Savior, God is pleased with us, not for anything we have ever done or could ever do, but because of what Jesus did for us. And because of His sacrifice, we don't have to worry about whether or not we are good enough...because Jesus is!

> For he hath made him to be sin for us, who knew no sin; that we might be made the righteousness of God in him. (2 Corinthians 5:21)

There was a time when I thought I had it all figured out. I was a fully grown, mature Christian woman, dining on the meat of the Word of God. A few people literally told me that they never worried about me because I "could never fall" because my foundation of faith was so strong. Be careful when people start telling you that. Your pride, and the devil, are just around the corner. The devil is always listening, and he's always up for a challenge. I don't say that to scare you. It's just a reality that we all need to know. Often, when it seems as if we're at the pinnacle of our faith, when it seems like we have it all figured out and we have come through the fire and made it to the other side victorious, that's when the devil goes on the offensive. Especially if we've let a bit of pride settle in.

That's the moment when we let our guard down, when we allow some chinks in the armor to appear. And trust me when I tell you that the devil is waiting with just the right ammunition to take you down if you're not on your guard. That's what happened to me. Remember the prayer I prayed out loud about my marriage in chapter 1? It was as if the devil had a Rolodex and was flipping through every single person from my past, looking for that one name of that one guy who might still be able to make me turn my head. At the time this happened, I had been in a committed relationship for over thirteen years. I wasn't always happy, but I was saved, I was in church leadership, and I thought I had it together. And I decided one night, probably after watching some movie about star-crossed lovers, that I could let my guard down and let my thoughts get away with me. I wasn't planning to actually *do* anything wrong; I was just going to play in the fire of my imagination, just a little "what if" scenario, one I thought would never actually happen.

I mean, God gave us an imagination, so what was wrong with escaping from my life for a little bit of time here and there to fantasize about a world where my life was different? What was wrong indeed. When you live in a fantasy world just a little bit here and there, what you're really doing is being unthankful. You're telling God that in spite of all of the wonderful, amazing things that He has blessed you with, that there could maybe be something better out there for you. Not more blessing but a different one (the trap).

So you let your guard down and you let your mind wander. After all, people are telling you how strong you are, right? And then you start thinking that if you could just pause your life for a moment and jump over into this other life, you would have exactly what you need. And it doesn't hurt thinking about it because it's *never* going to happen, right? That is one of the biggest, boldest, ugliest, debilitating lies from hell that you can ever fall for.

The life that God has given you…don't ever compare it to someone else's. Don't fantasize about a life you "could have" that's different. If you want a different life, and God's word is in line with pursuing the better life that you're wanting, then don't fantasize about it. Go for it. But make sure it's a fantasy you wouldn't mind sharing with God!

For example, it's not wrong to dream of a better job or a prettier home or better finances. But if the method for getting what you want isn't in line with His Word, it's not your life to dream about. You are coveting someone else's dream. And when it's not in line with His Word, you better stop imagining it, and you better run away as fast as you can and as far as you can because the devil is in the fine print! And there will be something to pay in the end.

That little thought that festers into a daydream explodes into your reality, supernaturally, and it will cost you so much more than you ever thought it could or should or would. And, the reality is, it could very likely break you. I know. It almost broke me. Honestly, it did break me. I nearly lost everything…my family, my friends, my church, my career, my health. It is still one of the worst pains I have ever experienced in my life, and saying I regret that very first thought doesn't even come close.

But God…

God is good and God is merciful, and God's mercy is new every morning. And I praise Him with all my heart for not leaving me bankrupt in that land of the dead that I put myself in, following after my own foolish fantasies cultivated by being unthankful.

Even as I struggle to finish this book, I am reminded I am who He says I am. Chosen…not forsaken. Doesn't matter the mistakes I've made in my life. Doesn't matter what I have or have not already accomplished. God put a story in my heart and a desire in my spirit to share that story with anyone willing to read it. And even now, as the devil tells me not to let anyone inside my life to see my skeletons, God is reminding me to bare my soul, even if it means owning the bones.

> Blessed be God, even the Father of our Lord Jesus Christ, the Father of mercies, and the God of all comfort; Who comforteth us in all our tribulation, that we may be able to comfort them which are in any trouble, by the comfort wherewith we ourselves are comforted of God. (2 Corinthians 1:3–4)

I'm a child of God. I've been forgiven. The slate has been washed clean. Not only has God forgiven me for every sin, His Word says He casts it as far as the east is from the west. Try to get an image of that in your mind. I mentally picture God winding up like a pitcher in the World Series, but when He lets that ball of my sins go, it doesn't stop at some arbitrary catcher's mitt behind home plate. Instead it goes up and out of the park, soaring into the sky and then into space, traveling faster and faster as it disappears into oblivion, never to be seen or remembered again.

Yet here comes the blame, the accusations, the condemnation, just when I'm down and vulnerable. But that isn't God. That's the accuser of the brethren, the angel of darkness who parades around as an angel of light, speaking lies and trying to steal our joy. I'm speaking of none other than Lucifer himself. And when that happens, you've just got to get an east–west baseball pitch point of view and say, "Not today, Satan. In fact, not *ever!*"

Stop letting the devil tell you that you can't come to God because you aren't good enough. You will categorically *never* be good enough. None of us ever will be. But the truth is, we don't have to be, because *He* already is! So stop wasting time wallowing in your guilt and shame. Lay it down. Pray for Jesus to come into your heart and forgive you. And then believe that He has. And the next time you fall down, and the devil starts telling you that you will never be good enough, just smile and remind him that you don't have to be, because Jesus already is!

> There is therefore now no condemnation to them which are in Christ Jesus, who walk not after the flesh, but after the Spirit. (Romans 8:1)

*****

Now it's your turn to play a little heavenly baseball.

- What nightmares of your past is the devil tormenting you about?

- What does God's Word say about it?

- Have you taken it to the cross?

- If so, did you lay it down, or are you still carrying it around with you, letting it play like a broken record in your mind?

- The Word says, "Rebuke the devil, and he will flee from you." What steps can you take to put him on the run?

- Take a moment to pray for God's grace over your sin, and record your thoughts and anything God speaks to you on the next page.

Quiet Reflections

LIE #4

I Can Have the Best of Both Worlds

The moment you get saved, the world looks different. You see things differently. You begin to think about things differently. You begin to realize there is a whole lot more to life than what you can see in front of you. This is especially true if you happen to be a teenager when you give your life to God. But part of seeing things differently is learning how to adjust to your new life. After all, as much as you have changed on the inside, the environment you live in hasn't changed with you, and that's when the struggle begins.

Because the world, your old world, does not want you to see things differently. It wants you to fit in, go with the flow, be like everyone else. And more than the world wants it, the devil wants it. The minute you get saved, the devil goes on the warpath because he knows he's most likely lost another soul for eternity. And since he's lost the power over your soul, the one thing he has left is to try to mess with your victory. He wants you to believe that you can't live out the same life that the early Christians lived, that the same level of discipleship doesn't exist anymore, and that you will be called a religious nut if you try to be different or stand out. Perhaps it's a little easier if your entire family is already walking in the faith (though numerous preachers' sons and daughters might say it's even harder).

But for me, it wasn't easy. In fact, becoming a Christian at the age of fourteen caused so many things to take place in my life. I wasn't prepared. I didn't have an anchor in my family to help guide me. My parents weren't atheists; they were just busy trying to survive this life themselves, trying to do it apart from God's guidance and shepherding. So really, all I had besides my newly found faith in Jesus was my church and my youth group.

In hindsight, that should have been enough, but if I'm being honest, I needed more. I needed stronger ties to Christianity in my home. I needed my church to support our youth leaders. I needed the members of my youth group to stay strong and help me stay strong. I needed a pastor to preach about temptation and how to avoid it. I needed to be grounded. I needed someone to be frank and honest with me about how the devil roams the earth seeking souls to devour. And I needed someone to tell me the secret to my success would be found only by spending time in the Word and on my knees, repenting when I failed, and trusting in my new relationship with Christ instead of all my seemingly important relationships with the world.

So I became a Christian, and the world came at me full force. At least, it seemed that way. At fourteen, it was all about being popular, liked, accepted. And for a Bible thumper in the 80s, there was a major disconnect between the two. It just wasn't "cool" to be religious in junior high; at least not in the circles I was familiar with. And then there were boys and hormones and social conventions and did I mention hormones?

So here you are, all nice and clean and washed in the blood of Jesus, eager to share your experience with everyone you know, and then the world, all wrapped up in pretty, shiny paper and bows presents itself to you. You lean on the church to guide you and your peers, but they can't be there in your mind to guide you 24/7. Plus, though you don't realize it at the time, your friends are fighting their own battles of peer pressure and temptation.

The Word says that when Jesus left the earth and ascended back up to heaven, He sent a comforter, the Holy Spirit, to guide us. And He does…when we listen. But with school, and sports, and summer jobs, and friends, and clothes, and boys (or, as an adult, work, family, finances, vacations, holidays…), it's easy to push God out, even accidentally. And when you begin pushing God out, the world pushes in. You've probably seen the experiment where they fill a large glass vase with sand (the world), and then rocks (important stuff to self), and then finally try to put the big things of God in with no room available. Then they switch things around and start in reverse, with the big things first, and everything miraculously fits with room left over. If you haven't ever seen this demonstrated, you should google it sometime. It's pretty profound. And once you figure out how to rearrange your priorities, it actually works. But most of us don't live that way. We live the first way, with work, bills, family activities, etc., first, trying to keep our heads above water while still trying to work in just a few minutes to pray and read a few verses in our Bible app. Sound familiar?

And before you know it, you are beginning to believe the next big lie of the devil. "I can have the world *and* Jesus." Well, yes…but *no*! The problem with this lie is that it is so close to the truth, it's too easy to believe and use to justify everything you choose to do with your life. It goes back to free will. When you get saved, you have Jesus, but you still live in the world. And the world wants you to believe that it has everything you could ever want or need, when in reality *Jesus* has everything you could want or need. That's why the Bible tells us that we are to be "in the world, not of it." It's also where the hymn comes from that proclaims, "This world is not my home." It's to remind us that we have to stay separate, and that's mighty hard to do when you don't have an anchor and life starts smacking you in the face from the moment your feet hit the floor in the morning.

For reasons I'd like to say were beyond my control, I didn't stay anchored long. And before I knew it, I was believing the lie that I could have both—Jesus and the world. The truth is, you just can't! Not without being miserable; not without making a lot of mistakes and having to live with a lot of guilt and regret; not without nearly losing your mind trying to serve two masters.

The truth is this world is *not* your friend. It doesn't want what's best for you. Instead, it wants to drag you back down into the same miry clay you escaped from when you first gave your life to Jesus, and it wants to convince you that you can be a Christian and love this life and the world at the same time. But believing that lie comes at a cost, a very high cost, and some people never find their way back. Or maybe they do, but it's after they've paid a lofty price for living a life "believing" in God but walking in the world, and they have the scars to prove it. I know I do.

> Be not deceived; God is not mocked: for whatsoever a man soweth, that shall he also reap. For he that soweth to his flesh shall of the flesh reap corruption; but he that soweth to the Spirit shall of the Spirit reap life everlasting. (Galatians 6:7–8)

I think I was sixteen when I first found myself walking more in the world than in Jesus. And I thought I was doing great. Boys were the only thing on my mind, other than possibly being popular. But where was Jesus? The truth is He was still very much there. He promises to never leave us or forsake us, and I could feel Him tugging at me, telling me not to do the things I was doing. I know this is true because I recorded it time and time again in the journals I kept all those years ago. But I chose to ignore His beckoning, and the more I did, the less I could hear Him, and the more loudly the world was shouting to come join it. And so, more and more, little by little, I did…and this book is filled with the fallout from those choices. The next chapter begins that journey. But before I go on, I want to tell *you* what I wished someone had told *me*!

1. Stay in the Word instead of playing around with the world.
2. Fan the flames of your relationship with Jesus or the flames of the world will burn your faith down to embers.
3. The world is not your friend. It will try to take your fire, your desire, and your relationship with Jesus.
4. Work on your relationship with Jesus *daily*!
5. If you find yourself drifting, get on your knees and repent and start again!

> And let us not be weary in well doing: for in due season we shall reap, if we faint not. (Galatians 6:9)

*****

So now as in previous chapters, it's your turn. Read through the five truths I just shared with you.

- What is God speaking to your heart right now? Do you feel Him tugging at you in some area of your life? Take a few minutes and pray for Him to reveal His truth to you.

- What did you discover? Is there something God wants you to change? If He's speaking to you, pray for strength and guidance in the area of concern.

- Do you have a specific time set aside daily to read the Word? A time to pray? Do you make time for worship?

- What else could you be doing to make your relationship with Him stronger?

- Finally, is there someone else you know who may be struggling with their relationship with God? Take a few minutes to lift them up in prayer, asking God to speak to their heart the way He's speaking to you. Record your thoughts on the next page.

Quiet Reflections

Lie #5

It's Too Late for Me

> What can wash away the guilty stain
> After all the wrong I've done?
> I've already tried a thousand ways,
> But it's never been enough.
> What could be enough?
> —Elevation Worship, "Better Word"

I've done too much and gone too far for God to love me. I have said that to myself so many times in my life, and each and every time, it was nothing more than a lie from the pits of hell! The Bible tells us differently.

> But God commendeth His love toward us,
> in that, while we were yet sinners, Christ died for
> us. (Romans 5:8)

If I had a nickel for every time I told myself this lie…well, let's just say I'd have plenty of nickels! You see, I gave my life to Jesus when I was fourteen, and then life happened, to put it straight to the point. I wasn't grounded in faith, and so though there were some early signs of fruit, the roots were not deep, and the soil was soon plagued with weeds and thorns. It didn't take long for the cares of this world (my desire to be popular) to override my commitment to

God, and by age eighteen, my life was a mess! I was a total wreck, and the condemnation I felt was so heavy, I didn't see how I could ever find my way back to God. Why would He even want a sinner like me anyway? I listened to that lie for nearly a decade!

I kept trying to "be good enough" to deserve to ask for forgiveness. Talk about an exercise in futility. First of all, if I couldn't be good enough not to fall into a sinful life, how was I supposed to be good enough while I was neck-deep *living* that sinful life? The truth is, I could *never* be good enough—*no one can*! For none of us "deserve" salvation (we are all sinners). It is God's gift to us, given freely to all who will partake of His goodness.

And this is exactly how the devil deceives people. He convinces us through guilt and condemnation that we've blown it—gone too far and done too much—and God doesn't want us. But this is one of the biggest lies the devil tells us. The Bible says, "For God so loved the world that He gave His only begotten Son [Jesus], that whosoever believeth in Him should not perish, but have everlasting life" (John 3:16). Not "whosoever is good enough," but whosoever believes in Him! I was a believer, so that made me a "whosoever." And here's the part the devil doesn't want people to see. Anyone who believes they've done too much for God to love them, by virtue of that confession, believes in God, so that makes them a "whosoever," too!

I feel something welling up inside of me, and I don't know where it's going to go, so I'm just going to start. I want to talk to you about abortion. Abortion is such a hot topic of division in our world today. In fact, if I'm not careful, I'm liable to say something on the topic that will lead me to either getting disowned by my prolife friends or having my book banned by the prochoice folks. Let me be really clear for a minute. This chapter is not a political statement. It's a heart statement. A very personal heart statement. And one that God needs some beautiful (but hurting) women to hear. Everyone makes mistakes. And whether you feel fine with your decision now or are already feeling a loss, the emptiness will come.

Somewhere in your life, if you've had or plan to have an abortion, you will have to deal with the aftermath from a decision like that, a decision to end another life. I'm not talking about the initial decision. The aftermath *will* come, maybe not now, but eventually it will. I'm talking about the emptiness inside you when the guilt finally hits, and unless you run from God until the day you die, you will one day have to reconcile with that guilt. And perhaps that's exactly why you are running. Maybe the whole reason you've decided you don't need God is because you are afraid to face that guilt.

I remember coming back to God after years of rebellious living. I remember confessing all my sins at the altar and asking God for forgiveness. I remember wanting to feel free. But I wasn't. I mean I was, because "whom He sets free is free indeed." But I didn't feel free. I felt shackled to choices I made that could never be undone, choices I now regret. Every time I tried to run free, the devil would tap me on the shoulder and say, "Yes, you're doing good now, but remember they don't know what you've done. And when they find out, if they find out…you won't be free anymore."

Have you heard that one? I heard it play like a broken record. Every time I would get back in church, back in the Word, and back into worshipping our Savior, there he was, that lying serpent! And he was always hell-bent on sabotaging my progress, telling me that I could only go so far before I would need to retreat. And so I *would* retreat before I found myself in a situation where I might have to reveal the truth about my past to someone else.

So here we go…honesty time. (Deep breath.) I had made the decision, more than once in my life, to have an abortion. It was my deepest, darkest secret, the one that as a Christian I was the most ashamed of, the secret I kept just between me and God. And the devil knew it was my kryptonite. It haunted me every single time I walked into the church. If you will allow me, I'd like to take a segue here before I talk about how I was delivered from the guilt and emptiness. I need to talk to believers about the language of love. I completely understand being prolife. I feel like I am prolife. I think I knew that even during the first abortion, when I was living that rebellious life I mentioned. I knew that what I was doing wasn't right. I don't need anyone to tell me that now.

But we need to be very careful about what we say as supporters of the prolife movement. If we go on a rant about "how could anyone kill an innocent little baby?" and "how horrible it is," do you understand what we are really saying? We are telling the young woman who has already had an abortion that she can't be loved. We are telling her that there is no hope. That Jesus could never love her because she has taken the life of her baby. Maybe that's not the message we intend to send, but that's the message she is receiving. Trust me, I remember. When you are shouting at someone to please not kill her baby, you are simultaneously condemning every woman who already has. It's a fine line. We condemn the act but love the person. But is that the message being received?

I was both amazed and aggravated by the announcement by the Roman Catholic Church that they had finally decided to forgive women who have had abortions. I'm sorry (and I don't mean to offend my Catholic friends), but who made the Pope, or the Catholic Church, or its priests God? What gives anyone the right to decide which sins can be forgiven and which ones can't? All sin is sin in God's eyes, and though it's about time that we get onboard with the acceptance that all sins can be forgiven, we need to remember that every act of rebellion is sin. There's no such thing as big sins and little sins in God's eyes. It's all under the blood when we give our hearts to Jesus. We also need to remember where mercy comes from.

Here's the truth. We are all sinners bound for hell if not for the grace of God through His Son Jesus Christ. That's all of us. And one sin does not deserve to be forgiven over another. The apostle Paul was persecuting and killing Christians, yet Jesus still sought him out and forgave him. Killing people for professing their faith in our Lord and Savior could be forgiven, but killing an unborn child couldn't? Seriously.

So now back to where I was going in the first place (segue finished; soapbox put away). I hope you are still reading, because this is where grace comes in. I'm here to tell anyone who's ever had an abortion, I know the lies the devil is telling you, and the guilt you are feeling way down deep inside where no one else knows you are hurting.

But I also know God truly loves you. And He is willing and ready to forgive you. And not just forgive you but give you the power to forgive yourself and replace all that emptiness with His love. All you have to do is ask for it. It's that simple. You don't have to spend your life feeling like you are outside of God's love. He wants to not only forgive you, He also wants to heal you, and He will…if you will let Him.

I needed someone to know that. God needed someone to know that. But as long as we keep shouting condemnation, those who have experienced an abortion will forever be afraid to face their guilt and pain and reach out for grace and healing.

God's desire is that *none* of us would perish, but rather that we would *all* come to a place of repentance and be partakers of His free gift of eternal life through Jesus Christ (2 Peter 3:9, paraphrased). No one is beyond redemption, and no one could ever go too far to be out of the reach of God's love…*no one!* Tell the devil he's a liar and embrace the "whosoever." Remember the thief on the cross? Not the one that blasphemed the Spirit but the one who recognized Jesus as the Son of God. He found forgiveness as he hung on a cross, crucified for his crimes. With his last breath, he reached out to the only one who could save him, and he found redemption. He was a "whosoever," too. And so are you! Won't you come?

Now it's your turn. What about you? Are you dealing with the pain and scars of abortion? Or perhaps something else, something equally painful that keeps you in a place of emptiness and regret. There is nothing you can't go to the Father with. And something else I'm learning: there's nothing that can hold you down, and no demonic kryptonite exists that can stop you from finding forgiveness and fulfilling your destiny.

*****

Take a few minutes and think about what you've read in this chapter.

- Is something bothering you right now? Will you face it and confess it to Jesus now? If not, what's holding you back?

- Do you know someone who is experiencing the pain of regret but seems too ashamed to talk about it? How can you minister to them? If it's you, who can you talk to and get ministered by?

- What mistakes, thoughts, or desires do you keep hidden in the secret chambers of your heart? Are you ready to let them go and find mercy instead?

- What would it feel like to be free? Record your thoughts in the space provided on the next page.

Quiet Reflections

LIE #6

God's Not Really All That Interested in Me

One of the biggest lies people believe is that the Creator isn't really concerned about our day-to-day lives. We are led to believe, in our society, that if there is a higher power, He has much more important things to do than to worry about us. But this ideology couldn't be further from the truth. I don't know how He does it, but God is very much tuned in to every aspect of our lives, from decisions we make, to what holds our attention, to the very number of hairs on our heads. We are His magnificent creation, His work of art! And just as a painter pays attention to every line and stroke of the brush, God is painting the masterpiece of our lives, allowing us to assist in the brushstrokes.

So what about this master painter, the Creator of the universe? To think that He looks down from His majesty on high and sees me, this rebellious, stubborn sinner? *Well, maybe when I really get something right or really commit some major sin…then He sees me. But the rest of the time, I'm just another ant in the anthill going about my day.* This lie is perhaps the easiest one to believe. Once you get to the point where you actually believe there is a God, one that created the heavens and the earth and all living creatures, it seems like He's much too busy running the universe to worry about us.

That's what we tell ourselves. Our daily lives, the daily choices we make, it doesn't really matter as long as we go to church, try to be nice to other people, and stay away from the "big sins." We can pretty much just live our lives. And maybe if we are lucky, we will get a sign somewhere along the way that God knows we are here, maybe a warm feeling as we sing worship songs or pray a little harder when we are in a rough spot. Then we might get to hear from Him and get a little more oil in our lamps to keep us burning. Right?

I wasted so many years of my life believing that. So much time wasted trying to figure this life out on my own. Struggling to find meaning, wondering if the things that have happened to me would ever make sense. Just waiting, I guess for the Rapture, because that's all there was. That's what I thought anyway. But that's not what my Bible says. And it's not what your Bible says either! The Word says that Jesus died to save us, but before He ascended, He said He would send the Comforter, the Holy Spirit, and that He would no longer dwell in tents made by man but would forever dwell in the hearts of men. Not just the holiest men, or the greatest men, but all men, the "whosoever" I talked about in the previous chapter.

So let's talk about that. I know what you're thinking. Let me ask you a question. Why is it so hard to believe He cares about you? Why does it seem impossible that He could be right here with you as you are reading this? I think it's because we don't really understand the character and nature of God. So let's look at what the Word tells us about the nature of God.

First, God is all-knowing.

> For if our heart condemns us, God is greater
> than our heart, and knoweth all things. (1 John 3:20)

He knows everything that has ever been and everything that will ever be. There is no barrier of time with God. One of my favorite pastors used to say, "We see to the corner, but God sees around the corner." That's pretty amazing when you think about it. We don't usually have a clue what is about to happen, but God always knows, and He is already planning His response.

> But as it is written, Eye hath not seen, nor ear heard, neither have entered into the heart of man, the things which God hath prepared for them that love him. (1 Corinthians 2:9)

Second, God is all-seeing.

> The eyes of the LORD are in every place, watching the evil and the good. (Proverbs 15:3)

He can see everything that is happening at any given moment all at the same time. Think about that for a minute. That means that while He sees the Pope addressing the masses, He also sees the widow down on her knees. While His Spirit is filling the church house with His presence on Sunday morning, He is also at the nursing home, touching the hearts of those who are praising Him from their wheelchairs and beds. That's pretty incredible.

> Nothing in all creation is hidden from God's sight. Everything is uncovered and laid bare before the eyes of Him to whom we must give account. (Hebrews 4:13)

Third, God is all-powerful. This one really gets me excited. All-powerful...that means *nothing* is more powerful than God! Not the storms of life, not death, not the devil himself.

> Behold, I am the Lord, the God of all flesh. Is there anything too hard for me? (Jeremiah 32:27)

Furthermore, God is always in control, always able to defeat the enemy. And when His spirit dwells inside us, we have access to that power. The Bible asks the question, "If God is for us, who can be against us?" (Romans 8:31). Think about that for a moment. You may be asking how we know that God is for us. That same chapter of Romans goes on to explain. When you have time, read Romans 8, the whole chapter. It speaks so much about God's power and how He exercises that power toward us.

> He that spared not his own Son, but delivered him up for us all, how shall he not with him also freely give us all things?... Nay, in all these things we are more than conquerors through him that loved us. (Romans 8:32, 8:37)

Now, ask yourself, if God is all-knowing, all-seeing, and all-powerful, is it really that hard to believe that He knows what is going on in your life from one moment to the next? And since He does know, doesn't it stand to reason that He would be concerned about you as an individual? Ponder that for a moment. Block out the lies the world (and the devil) has been telling you, and let the truth fill your heart and mind, and then think about your life for a few moments. Can you think of a time when the only explanation for what happened was that God was there? If you can't, that's okay. We will come back to that in a later chapter. But I have a feeling that if you really thought about it, you'd think of a time when there just was no other explanation. It had to be God!

I don't remember when I first knew, when I really understood, that God is indeed concerned about my daily life. I know there had to be a moment that it clicked because I remember not thinking He cared (the lie), and I remember countless years that have gone by in which He has revealed to me, both through His Word and in my life experiences, just how much He does care. I also know that there is a big—nay, *huge* difference in my day when I don't make time for fellowshipping with Him. Nowadays, I do my best to invite Him along with me everywhere I go. I mean, He's going to come along anyway, but I find I make better choices when I remember He's there.

On the subject of spending time with God, now that you realize just how invested in your life God really is, there's something you can do to make that relationship even better. You're probably thinking, *He's already saved me, and now I know He cares about me. What could be better than that?* This is my favorite part about God, and the part the devil really doesn't want you to know about.

At the same time that God is this amazing creator of the universe, this unfathomable, merciful savior to the world, our heavenly Father who watches over us and cares about every part of us, there's yet another characteristic of God that still overwhelms and floods my soul. He also desires to be our friend. And a *real* friend, not some fair-weather, "see you around when there's something I need" friend but a true, "never leave you, never forsake you," "love you like a brother or sister" friend.

That's the character of God we find in the resurrected Savior, Jesus. He's as real a friend as you want Him to be, and as true a friend as you could ever find anywhere else. But as I mentioned before, He's also a gentleman.

For any relationship to work (and that's what this is, a relationship), there has to be frequent time set aside for intimacy. I say "set aside" because intimacy has to be planned and created. It doesn't just happen. You have to make time to get alone with God, to listen to His instruction, and garner wisdom from His Word. It has to resonate in your mind, become more than words on a page. It's the living, breathing Word (Christ Jesus).

The more of Him we take into our hearts daily, the less room we have for the muck and the mire of the ungodly world we live in today. And the more time we spend with our friend Jesus, the more we begin to realize how He's always been there, through everything. Sometimes He walks along beside us, encouraging us to keep going. Sometimes He walks ahead of us to help us avoid the pitfalls of life. And sometimes we realize we aren't walking at all. That's when He carries us. Those are the hardest times. Remember that question I asked you earlier, to think of a time when you knew it had to be God? For me, those are the times when I realize He had been carrying me. Otherwise, I would have never made it through. Yeah…that's my Jesus. And to think, once upon a time I told myself that He wasn't really all that interested in me. Now it's your turn.

*****

- How would you rate your relationship with God? Is there anything missing?

- Do you desire more from God than you have now? If you could ask Him for anything, what would it be?

- What lies has the devil told you about how much God loves you?

- Get alone by yourself and ask God to reveal His character to you.

- Ask Him to help you understand who He is and who He wants to be in your life.

- Record what He reveals to you in the space provided on the next page.

Quiet Reflections

LIE #7

You Should Just Believe in Yourself

Lie: "We should take pride in our accomplishments and talents. It is good to have pride in yourself and others." (Stay with me. This is an extra sneaky one.)

Having confidence isn't a bad thing. We all need some level of confidence to step out in our faith. But where that confidence comes from and who gets the glory is what separates the truth from the lie. God wants us to have every confidence in Him, in His love for us, His promise to never leave us or forsake us, and the promise of grace and an eternity in heaven. In fact, the concept of faith (believing without seeing) is rooted in that confidence. But it's confidence in God, not self.

The devil has spun such a tricky lie that we've even created a word for it: *self*-confidence. Self-confidence is a feeling of trust in one's own abilities, qualities, and judgment. A self-confident person doesn't need to rely on anyone else to make it. Yet throughout the scriptures, God shows us that His plan is for us to realize how much we need Him and to learn to depend on and trust in Him completely. There's no room for self!

> For thou shalt worship no other god: for the
> Lord, whose name is Jealous, is a jealous God.
> (Exodus 34:14)

> Therefore, turn thou to thy God: keep mercy and judgment, and wait on thy God continually. (Hosea 12:6)

> Trust in the Lord with all thine heart; and lean not unto thine own understanding. In all thy ways acknowledge him, and he shall direct thy paths. Be not wise in thine own eyes: fear the Lord, and depart from evil. (Proverbs 3:5–6)

The opposite of trusting God is trusting self. And trusting self is being prideful. I'd almost bet you are ready to skip this chapter or maybe even throw the whole book across the room right now. I know I struggled with writing it. Nobody wants to admit they are too prideful. One might say we have "too much pride" to admit it. Ironic, really. The truth is God *hates* pride. And it's the very thing the devil enjoys using against us the most! Let's examine some more verses.

> [Things the Lord hates:] A proud look, a lying tongue, and hands that shed innocent blood. (Proverbs 6:17)

> Pride goeth before destruction, and a haughty spirit before a fall. (Proverbs 16:18)

> Every way of a man is right in his own eyes, but the Lord pondereth the hearts. (Proverbs 21:2)

> A high look, and a proud heart, and the plowing of the wicked, is sin. (Proverbs 21:4)

I could go on and on…

Pride is defined as inordinate self-esteem; an unreasonable conceit of superiority; disdainful treatment of others as beneath you.

- Pride is what caused Lucifer's rebellion.
- Pride is what caused Eve to eat the apple.
- Pride is what caused the Israelites to wander in the wilderness.
- And pride is what leads us to rebellion against God and His commandments and to step out in faith in our own strengths and abilities instead of relying on God to guide us.

Whew! Are you still with me? Good! Keep reading…

I've been prideful on so many occasions throughout my life, sometimes in big ways and sometimes in what seem like little insignificant ways. I'm realizing even as I'm working on editing this chapter, I've been struggling with pride. I don't mean to be prideful. I try to stay humble. But yesterday was frustrating, and I stepped up in a good way, and then today I was bragging about it. Wow! Didn't even see it!

I don't mean to sound harsh or like I'm trying to come down on the little things. That's not my purpose in this book at all. The truth is all of us have an issue with pride. It's part of what makes us human. The bottom line is still the same. When we lean to our own understanding and trust in what we can do (forgetting to follow God's leading), we are walking on dangerous ground. Did you notice in both Proverbs 21:4 and Proverbs 6:17, how King Solomon lists pride on the same level as "the plowing of the wicked" and "hands that shed innocent blood"?

King Solomon learned some hard lessons himself about pride and arrogance, as I'm sure all of us have. Pride sneaks in disguised as self-esteem and confidence, and before you know it, you are looking down on someone else, judging another's actions, or feeling envy over something someone else got that you thought you deserved. It even happened to me right there on the church pew a few months ago, and I had to repent! It is one of the things God hates most, and one of the things the devil likes to use to trip us up as often as he can.

It's a constant struggle for me, not because I'm so self-confident, but because in reality, in many ways, I'm not! I spent a better part of my childhood being moved from town to town, school to school, always being bullied and never staying long enough to develop deep roots. My self-esteem was so distorted. I usually found myself overcompensating by being extremely prideful in the few things I felt I could brag about (one of the primary reasons I got picked on, most likely). That and the fact that some kids are just plain mean! But I digress…maybe another book for another day.

As I grew older, my issues with self-confidence (lack of) and low self-esteem caused me to spend a lot of my time seeking the approval of others. And anytime I found that I was getting a lot of approval from others in a particular area, self-consciousness turned to confidence, which eventually turned to pride. There's that word again.

It's an issue I continually have to battle. God wants us to walk in confidence, but it needs to be confidence in Him, in what He can do for us, and in how much we need Him. That's what the scripture means when it says He's a jealous God. He wants all our adoration and praise, all our trust, all our heart, mind, soul, and strength. All of it!

> Blessed are the meek: for they shall inherit the earth. (Matthew 5:5)

> Humble yourself in the sight of the Lord and He will lift you up. (James 4:10)

> And whosoever shall exalt himself shall be abased; and he that shall humble himself shall be exalted. (Matthew 23:12)

*****

You may not be ready to examine your life for pride right now. But I encourage you to reflect just a little. Look at your most recent social media posts. Your last five text messages.

- Think about your last conversation with a coworker. Is there evidence of your faith in God and what He's doing in your life? Or is it faith (pride) in self?

- What are you being prideful about? It may be something really big or something you see as minor. Either way, remember that God hates pride! But He loves you.

- Take a minute to pray and ask God to show you areas in your life where you are being prideful. When He reveals it to you, surrender it. Ask Him to forgive you for it. Then get it out of your life! Blessings await you on the other side.

Quiet Reflections

LIE #8

I Can't Forgive That Person

"There are some people I just can't forgive."

I've heard that a thousand times. I've said it a few hundred times myself. The truth is, there will be people in your life that hurt you, often in ways that other people can't fathom. You don't think anyone else could possibly understand how deep the pain goes or how much of an impact the scars have on your life. But there is One who does understand, who sees deep within your heart to the pain that festers and gnaws at you, the thing that brings you nightmares, anxiety, distrust of letting others get too close to you, the thing that defines everything else you do and the choices you make, your filter in life.

The One who not only sees the pain but also feels that pain with you is Jesus.

So you are asking yourself, "If Jesus understands my pain, He knows how deep the wound is. So how could He possibly expect me to forgive that person?" The fact of the matter is, He wants you to forgive because *you need* to let it go. That's the only way to heal, to rebirth that part of your heart, to be whole again.

When Jesus tells us to forgive, it's rarely ever about the other person. Granted, we are all sinners in need of grace and forgiveness, and that person needs it just as much as anyone else, but we are to work out our own salvation with fear and trembling, right? So we aren't going to focus on the other person right now. We are going to focus on what matters: our own heart and walk with Jesus.

You've heard the scripture "God is love." And you've probably also heard the scripture "Love never fails." Well, if God is love, and love never fails, then it's safe to say God never fails. And we already knew that, right? But unfortunately, *people* do fail, often miserably. And when someone hurts you, he or she has failed you. Have you ever wondered why? Think about that for a moment. I do not believe that people are born with the mindset of "How can I make someone else miserable today?" Or "What can I do to make sure I cause someone else insufferable pain this week?" It's just not in our DNA (remember, we were created in the image of God).

So, if we aren't born to go around hurting people, what happened? I am reminded of a picture frame I cut my finger on yesterday. It was shoved down in a box, and when I tried to force another frame in beside it, my hand slipped between them, and I ended up with a pretty nasty and painful gash on the backside of my middle finger. In fact, it still hurts today, especially when I bump up against something with it.

Let's start with the frame. When it was created, it was designed to hold and display a large photo (10x13 inches). The frame was designed to add a decorative touch to the photo while the glass partition was designed to protect the photo from damage. So this frame was created to both display and protect its contents. However, over the last two years, it's merely been packed away in a box with twenty other picture frames, gathering dust and rusting.

When I took it out of the box and took away the newspaper wrapped around it for protection, I exposed its vulnerability but also its hidden beauty. But then instead of hanging it on the wall, I placed it, on its edge (for my convenience), in another box, to be left to gather more dust and rust, and began adding other frames next to it, packing them tightly together. Then I attempted to squeeze one more frame in, and that was it, the frame couldn't take it and it shifted, exposing the now fragile edge of the glass, cutting a gash in the part of my hand closest to it.

Now, did that frame intentionally hurt me? If I had been using it for its intended purpose, would it have cut me? If it had been properly cared for in the past, would the glass have had such a sharp edge exposed? If I hadn't been putting so much pressure on it, would it have shifted and cut me? The answer to all those questions is *no*!

Now take a deep breath and imagine if that frame were another person, with hopes and dreams, thoughts and feelings. Now walk through that passage again and think about the condition of the "heart" of the frame. It didn't intend to hurt me. It wasn't designed to hurt me. It was designed to be beautiful. But because of its life experiences, it was positioned in such a way that when I came in contact with it, it hurt me.

Now shift your focus to my finger for a few minutes. When I came in contact with the picture frame, I actually had good intentions. I was cleaning out the garage and trying to consolidate boxes of my mom's things we have in storage while getting rid of spider nesting places. I unwrapped the picture frames because spiders love to hide in the newspapers. I was placing the frames on their sides so they wouldn't get pressed on and break (like some of the ones on the bottom had). I thought I was being careful to place the frames in the new box, but I also wanted to fit them all, so I put them a little too close together. And when I attempted to crowd one more in, that's when my hand slipped, and my finger was cut by the frame.

So the frame caused me pain, a lot of pain, and I will most likely have a small scar on my finger because of it. But here's the reality. The frame wasn't designed to hurt me. I wasn't planning to be hurt by it, but past decisions and experiences, as well as the current environment, caused the frame to be in a position to hurt me, and hurt me it did. And the frame isn't going to come back and ask me to forgive it either. So I can throw it away, leave it packed forever, or, eventually, I can take it out, dust it off, and hang it on the wall. The choice is mine, and with time, the finger will heal, and the scar will fade some.

I could be afraid of that frame. I could be so worried about getting cut again that I never touch it again. But I'd be missing something. 'Cause you see, there's a picture inside that frame, a picture of someone I care about, and it was an image someone cared enough about to put it in a frame to begin with. So if I never go back and pull that frame out, I won't ever see that picture again.

Also, if I don't let myself get over the cut and the pain, I might decide to never touch another picture frame again, and I'd miss out on all kinds of images that way. No, the best thing I can do is let go.

Forgive the frame for hurting me. Try to understand that for it to be in a position or attitude to hurt me, something had to have happened to cause it to be that way, because frames aren't designed to be dangerous.

*****

Yes, it's just a frame. But imagine a person who's hurt you.

- What have they been through in their own life to cause them to be in a position to hurt you?

- What have you done, if anything, that put you in the position to be hurt by them? Was it *really* completely their fault?

- Does it matter in retrospect of the vastness and eternity of time? Is it worth hanging on to the pain?

- Yes, sometimes forgiveness is hard, but it's also so therapeutic and freeing. Only one question this time. You know who you need to forgive. What are you waiting on?

Quiet Reflections

Side Note

Even as I write this, I can feel the time growing short. We don't have nearly as much time as we think we do. The antichrist is gathering his armies, and his spirit is flooding the minds of the lost faster than we can imagine. The lines have been drawn between good and evil, and many people have found themselves standing on the wrong side. As we approach the last days, we need to be fully aware of the Word of God and what it says. We need to let it speak life into our situations, to bring us clarity and understanding for the lies the devil presents. It's going to be too late when we realize that we were standing on the wrong side of things because we chose to be blinded from the truth. It is now that we must open our eyes and see things for what they are. The devil is a liar and he has crafted such a masterpiece of deception, such that even the elect are beginning to be deceived. God will not be mocked. The truth is still the truth and the truth shall set you free. But you have to be willing to see the truth for what it is. There's so much deception in the world now that people don't know what to believe. Believe the Word of God. Believe the Bible. Believe the Holy Spirit. Anything that doesn't align is deceit and lies from the devil.

PART 2

God's Truths

TRUTH #1

Eternity Is a Choice

I've heard it my whole life, the argument people use to run from God. *How could a loving God send anyone to hell?* It's a fair question, but hidden beneath the surface is one of the greatest truths in the Bible. The quick answer is He doesn't. He won't. The Word says that God wants none to perish but for all to find salvation in Jesus Christ. And *all* can! So what's this business about hell, then? How do people end up there if God doesn't send them?

> If we say that we have no sin, we deceive ourselves, and the truth is not in us. If we confess our sins, he is faithful and just to forgive us our sins, and to cleanse us from all unrighteousness. (1 John 1:8–9)

> For if after they have escaped the pollutions of the world through the knowledge of the Lord and Savior Jesus Christ, they are again entangled therein, and overcome, the latter end is worse with them than the beginning. For it had been better for them not to have known the way of righteousness, than, after they have known it, to turn from the holy commandment delivered unto them. But it is happened unto them accord-

> ing to the true proverb, the dog is turned to his own vomit again; and the sow that was washed to her wallowing in the mire. (2 Peter 2:20–22)
>
> Knowing this first, that there shall come in the last days scoffers, walking after their own lusts, And saying, Where is the promise of his coming? for since the fathers fell asleep, all things continue as they were from the beginning of the creation. For this they willingly are ignorant of, that by the word of God the heavens were of old, and the earth standing out of the water and in the water. (2 Peter 3:3–5)
>
> Ye therefore, beloved, seeing ye know these things before, beware lest ye also, being led away with the error of the wicked, fall from your own stedfastness. (2 Peter 3:17)

This is the part where I get frustrated the most. God has this wonderful plan for all of us to spend eternity with Him in paradise. His Word says that he doesn't want anyone to miss out on this eternity. But sadly, there will be many who do. The Bible says that narrow is the gate (to heaven) and few are those who find it. Wide is the gate that leads to destruction. And it's not because He makes it so hard for anyone to find their way to the narrow gate. It's because people choose not to find it. And that's the frustrating part.

Whether it's through foolish pride or having been offended by someone who claims to be a member of the faith or just selfish free will, I just don't get it. God offers this free, wonderful gift to anyone who is willing to accept it. His only request is that we acknowledge the birth, life, death, and resurrection of His Son, Jesus Christ. And that in faith, we surrender our will to His and ask Him to save us.

> The Lord is not slack concerning his promise, as some men count slackness; but is longsuf-

fering to us-ward, not willing that any should
perish, but that all should come to repentance.
(2 Peter 3:9)

It's simply a matter of asking for forgiveness for being less than perfect. Which, by the way, all of us are. The Bible says that none are perfect, all have fallen short, all have sinned, save one, our Savior Jesus Christ. Why is it so hard for people to accept that? Why is it so hard to believe that a loving Creator would make a way for all His creation to share an eternal bliss?

We can't say that it's because we don't believe that a loving God would do that, because the number one argument people have against God is how He could send people to hell. The very argument contradicts their excuse.

I remember the first time that I heard the gospel when I was old enough to really understand the message. Jesus died for me. Because of the fall of Adam, we are all under the curse of sin. It's part of our free will. God made a way for us to be reunited with Him. He made a way to overcome the curse of one man, Adam, through the blood sacrifice of one man, one perfect lamb, Jesus. What is so difficult about that?

Jesus doesn't tell us we have to be a certain level of good or that we have to do a certain number of good works. He doesn't say that we have to be perfect. In fact, He says the opposite. He knows that we need Him. That's why He died for us. Because we need a Savior. And He beckons all of us to come. He offers salvation freely to everyone who will come.

Why would anyone choose to deny that gift and live this life apart from Jesus, as hard as this life is? Why would anyone want to live a life without hope for what's next? Why would anyone want to take a chance on spending eternity in hell simply because their pride or their guilt or their shame keeps them from acknowledging their need for a savior?

To me it's the definition of insanity. Has the devil so deceived the world that people really think that this life is all there is? And then when you die, it's over? How does that even make sense? It just makes me sad. None of us are promised tomorrow, or even the next hour. But what we do with the time we have left determines our eternity!

*****

Now it's your turn. Think about what you just read. Search out other scriptures that mention eternal life. Then ask yourself…

- Do you believe that God wants anyone to go to hell?

- Do you believe that eternity is a choice?

- Have you decided to follow Jesus?

- If not, ask yourself, what's holding you back?

Quiet Reflections

TRUTH #2

His Grace Is Sufficient

This is one of those chapters where you really need to read to the end, or you'll miss the point. It's not about how badly we've failed but rather how good God's grace is.

Just about everyone is familiar, at least to some extent, with the Ten Commandments. *Lifetime* television loves to air the old Charlton Heston movie from the 1950s, my husband's personal favorite. But for the most part, there seems to be about three camps of opinions on the Ten Commandments in modern days.

One camp believes it to be an honored tradition to keep them posted on monuments in front of or framed inside historical buildings across our nation. Another group believes them to be outdated and even offensive, given the norms of present-day America, and demand they be removed from every public place, in an attempt to wipe them out of existence. And still yet, a third camp likes to recite one or more of the commandments as needed to make a point or be condescending toward others.

But I wonder how long it has been since the average person, even the average God-fearing churchgoer, has stopped and really thought about the importance of the Ten Commandments and its application to our walk with Christ today.

I was a God-fearing churchgoer, and yet I never really thought about it much. Oh sure, I knew them. One God, don't kill, don't steal, honor parents, etc., all the things we "live by," kind of the golden rules of all rules. But how did they fit in with my life with Christ? With so much of the Old Testament ways having been replaced (upgraded) by Jesus's life, death, and resurrection (the New Covenant), just how applicable are the Ten Commandments anyway? Well, I would say they are very applicable. Let me explain.

The most important commandment that God gives us, according to Jesus, is "Thou shalt love the Lord thy God, with all thy heart, with all thy soul, and with all thy mind." God didn't just say to believe in Him. He said we are to *love* Him, and even more than that, we are to love Him with *all* our heart, *all* our soul, and *all* our mind. What does that mean? What does it look like in our daily life?

Many Christians barely go to church, let alone spend time in prayer, praise, and worship, sometimes going a whole week without opening a Bible or lifting up their voice in prayer. I have seen so many places of *worship* where multiple members of the congregation show up late, just in time to hear the sermon, and then slip out before the altar call begins. I would ask what they are afraid of, but I think I already know the answer.

If they start singing songs of worship, or stick around for the altar call, they might actually have to deal with the gentle tugging of their hearts to do and be more! Way too many are just fine with putting in an appearance and then ducking out before they really start feeling God's presence. Is this loving God with *all* your heart, *all* your soul, and *all* your mind? Not even close!

And I get it, I do! I've been there. Your life is going along just fine, your friends and colleagues respect that you attend a weekly service, but you're not one of those "Bible-thumpers" like so many in society like to talk about. You're in a safe place, sitting straddled between two worlds. You've checked the box for eternal salvation, and you are good to go. No need to venture into the water any further, right?

Read the first commandment again before you answer that question. Does your current situation and depth of relationship with God feel sufficient, or are you starting to wonder if maybe you need to step it up a notch? A good place to start? Try getting to church *early* and singing the songs, directing your worship to God (not the worship team). Stay through the sermon, taking notes. Then during the altar call, instead of sneaking out ahead of the crowd, try *standing still* and listening to your heart to see if you just might feel a gentle tugging. And then *respond* to it. That's the Holy Spirit speaking to you. Don't be afraid to see what's waiting for you on the other side of submission! I guarantee you that it's a decision you'll never regret! Can I get an *amen* from folks who know what I'm talking about?

Let's move on to the second, and equally important, part of that commandment. "Thou shalt not have any other gods before Me." Hmmm…Netflix, houses, cars, careers, money, spouse and kids… The question I have to ask myself every single day is what percentage of my time and resources do I give to God each day relative to how much time I devote to everything else I just mentioned.

Now, I just want to make a disclaimer here. I am *not* against watching Netflix (I love my shows as much as anyone), and I'm not against a person having a career, a nice home, a sweet ride, a spouse that makes them incredibly happy, or enough money to keep all those things safe and secure. Whew! Glad I got that out of the way. But if we are putting those things before our relationship with God, then it becomes a problem, and it's a problem that will creep up on you, and you won't even notice it!

And you are robbing yourself of some of the most amazing blessings from God when He isn't first priority in your life. Missing out on all God has for you would be like winning the lottery for millions of dollars, and then being content when they only send you a check for a thousand dollars! And no, I'm not exaggerating. I could write an entire book on how many times and in how many ways God has blessed me, my family, and others around me. (Hmmm… perhaps I will someday!)

But back to the commandment. Let's talk about our favorite person for a few minutes… Self! We all like to talk about ourselves, right? I'll be honest. I am just as fond of it as anyone else. I'll be in a conversation, listening to someone tell me all about some experience they've just had. I'll get eager to share a similar experience, and then before I know it, I am totally monopolizing the conversation! It's something I really have to work on, not being consumed in my own experiences all the time. If you are honest, would you be willing to admit that describes you, too? Yup, that's what I thought! So, let's talk about "self" for a moment, and then we will circle back to the commandment.

Take a quick inventory of your daily life. Has taking care of yourself and your own needs become a god to you? How much time do we spend each day promoting self? Improving self? Beautifying self? Trying to win the approval from others of ourselves? Take a few minutes and ponder each of those things...

TikTok, slow-motion selfies, filters, apps, programs, support groups, beauty regimens, gym memberships, time in front of the bathroom mirror...any of that sound familiar? Though I can't relate to all of it, I definitely enjoy going to the gym and taking selfies (angles are my friend). In fact, I love working out. It brings me all kinds of happiness to get in a good workout and leave some sweat on the gym floor, especially if I've got an awesome playlist going on my phone. But there was a time a few years ago when I was *so* into working out that I realized it had become the major focus of my time. That and constantly sharing (bragging about) my progress in fitness and weight loss. I told myself I was being an inspiration to others, and that isn't completely untrue. I was doing great things for my physical health.

But there was a problem. I had gotten so caught up in my workout routines, my eating habits, getting the right nutrition, counting macros, checking my weight fifty times a day, etc., that I had slowly but surely dwindled my once active prayer life and Bible study time down to quick, "get it done" acts of nothing more than going through the motions. I was completely floored the day I realized that my body and my gym had become my god!

You see, the truth is, if we spent even half as much of our time building a relationship with God as we do taking care of self, we would have the most glorious spiritual gardens ever! And remember, I'm preaching to myself here as much as anyone. I did finally find a balance between working out and reading my Bible, but it's still just too easy to let those little selfie (selfish) gods sneak back into my daily life. Anyone know what I mean?

For example, I say I'm just going to play on social media for a few minutes before diving into my prayer and worship time. Next thing I know, an hour has passed, I'm sleepy, and my desire (willpower) to spend time in relationship building with the Father has disappeared, sucked through a hidden window of fulfilling selfish desires. Or I'll decide I'm just going to watch one more episode of my latest binge, only to end up watching hours of episodes until I'm so sleepy, I just give up and go to bed, leaving prayer time for another day. I always go to sleep on those occasions promising I'll do better tomorrow. And then the guilt comes, and I find myself apologizing to God for wasted time yet again.

I am so bad about this even now! I can't tell you how many game apps I have had to delete from my cell phone because I become addicted to "just one more game" or, most recently, "just one more pixel picture to complete!" And I can actually picture God sitting up there in heaven looking down on me, sadly shaking His head as I blow off yet another prayer date with my Savior, thinking about how many times He's reminded me, "Thou shalt have no other gods before me."

But God is gracious and forgiving. Sometimes it's easy to take that for granted, forgetting to show reverence for the Holy Creator, who's so much bigger than I tend to imagine. Sometimes He has to give me a little nudge on occasion, and when I really need it, something more like a metaphorical two-by-four to my head, just to remind me that I'm letting another mini-god creep into my heart unawares. And then I have to stop, repent, and try to get things back on track. I'm so grateful He's a merciful and loving God!

> O taste and see that the Lord is good: blessed is the man that trusteth in him. O fear the Lord, ye his saints: for there is no want to them that fear him. (Psalm 34:8–9)

Grab yourself a quick refill on your favorite beverage (mine is coffee), and let's take a quick look at some of the other Commandments.

"Remember the Sabbath and keep it holy." How many people actively do this anymore? Our culture has rooted in us the ideology of "gotta work more, earn more, do more, go, go, go…no rest for the weary…" We spend so much time cramming more stuff into our week that it spills over into our day off, to the point that we end up saying "Sabbath what?"

Life will keep you busy if you let it, and while God does honor a person with a strong work ethic (after all, He created the whole world and everything in it in less than a week), He also "rested the seventh day." What many people don't understand is that the Sabbath was given to us as a gift, a reminder that we all need to stop and rest, take a deep breath, and appreciate God's provisions and what we've accomplished for the week. But with the hustle and bustle of our world today, sometimes it takes a concerted effort to remember to take a day of rest.

This is why God made it one of His commandments to *honor* the Sabbath day and keep it holy! Don't forget to purposefully build in a day of rest to your busy schedule. If you can't devote a whole day, start out slow, maybe an hour a day, where you just slow down, quiet your spirit, and spend time with God, just resting in all His blessings and provisions. And if you struggle with this, ask God to help you learn how to develop the Sabbath spirit in your routine. He's a good God, and He loves it when His children ask Him for help to live a more godly life!

"Thou shalt not commit adultery." Hold your hat and your heart! This is a tough one (tougher than some may think). What does society feed us? Things like "but everyone is doing it, and besides you don't need marriage to be committed, right?" And "how will you know if you are compatible if you don't give it a test drive first?" You have to admit, sexuality sells and it's *everywhere!*

Music, TV, movies, next door, at work…we can't go anywhere anymore without seeing something with sexual connotations. Just about every single popular movie has one or more sexually explicit scenes and/or conversations. Music lyrics are full of references to sex. TV shows flaunt sexual relationships outside of marriage.

Advertisements utilize the most attractive people in the most revealing attire to sell their products. And now just about everywhere you go, you see people making out in public or wearing clothes that simply don't leave enough to the imagination.

We allow these things to exist because we enjoy them; maybe not *all* of them, but everyone has their favorites. For me, I have always enjoyed watching the original Patrick Swayze version of *Dirty Dancing*. It seems so harmless, right? A little bit of hugging and kissing while listening to some romantic music or watching a romantic movie, and before you know it…you've broken the commandment.

Think not? Think you have more control than that? Think I'm being too harsh? In Matthew 5:27–28, Jesus said, "You have heard that it was said, 'Do not commit adultery.' But I tell you that anyone who looks at a woman lustfully has already committed adultery with her in his heart." So, what am I doing when I watch *Dirty Dancing* and see Swayze with his shirt off? Yup…guilty!

What about you? Anything you need to stop and confess? Thankfully, as with the other commandments, God is merciful and willing to forgive us as many times as we mess up, especially since the temptation is literally everywhere these days!

Okay, okay. I hear you. You get the message. So I'll just briefly share a few thoughts on the other commandments and then get to the heart of this chapter: His grace!

"Thou shalt not steal." According to the book of Malachi, anytime we don't tithe, we are stealing from God, as well as any time we are lazy at work, where we are getting paid with the expectation of earning it, when we are actually playing on our phones or computers instead. Ouch!

"Thou shalt not covet." How much time, money, and energy do we spend keeping up with the Joneses? Better car, better house, better job, better spouse. We buy on credit rather than saving for it because we gotta have it now! We trade a perfectly good item for a new one just because we want it. We leave one partner to pursue another because the grass looks greener on the other side. Ouch! Ouch! Ouch!

"Thou shalt not kill." Abortion, which is the ending of a baby's life inside the womb, is legal, and people are losing their minds over the fear

of it becoming illegal again. Before you think I'm being condescending, be sure you've read my chapter on my own experiences with abortion.

"Thou shalt honor thy mother and thy father." Where should I start? Nursing homes are filled with people who have been abandoned by their families, too busy to take care of them. Before you crucify me for that statement, I know there are times when a parent has to go to a nursing home, and that not everyone who is in a nursing home is abandoned by their children. But if I struck a nerve, it might be time to go visit them! Additionally, kids all over the country are talking back to their parents, heirs are fighting over their inheritance, adult siblings are at war or not speaking to one another at all. Family members are bitter about old grievances. And if not any of that, then people are just simply too busy living their own lives to spend time with the ones who gave them life!

My point is that we are all guilty of breaking one or more of the commandments, and the Bible is clear about sin. All have sinned. And sin is sin. The Word says if you break even the smallest of the commandments, you are guilty of breaking the law. And it's nearly impossible to live on this earth without breaking some laws here and there. The Word says,

> And hereby we do know that we know him, if we keep his commandments. He that saith, I know him, and keepeth not his commandments, is a liar, and the truth is not in him. But whoso keepeth his word, in him verily is the love of God perfected: hereby know we that we are in him. He that saith he abideth in him ought himself also so to walk, even as he walked. (1 John 2:3–6)

> By this we know that we love the children of God, when we love God, and keep his commandments. For this is the love of God, that we keep his commandments: and his commandments are not grievous. For whatsoever is born of God overcometh the world: and this is the vic-

tory that overcometh the world, even our faith.
(1 John 5:2–4)

I could continue but hashing out all the ways that we (yes, me, too) have broken one or more of God's commandments is not really the point of this chapter. I had to go there to make my next point. I'll be honest. As I look over the list, I realize I have broken every single one of God's commandments, many of them as a repeat offender. Before I found Jesus, I was a sinner bound for hell. In fact, I was on a trajectory to bust hell wide open. If you don't believe me, you might need to go back and read some of my previous chapters.

But hallelujah, praise Jesus! His grace is sufficient! No matter what I did or will ever do, no matter how many commandments I have broken time and time again, Jesus is inside of me, and His Word is clear: "His grace is enough." When Jesus, the perfect lamb, hung on the cross, He made a way for us to receive forgiveness for every sin we have ever committed or will ever commit, as long as we have a repentant heart and faith in His power and desire to forgive us.

Nothing is too big for Him. Nothing surprises Him. No one is beyond redemption. As my pastor used to say, that should make a hypocrite shout! God is so good to us. His mercy is new every single morning. And He knew before the world began that we would need a Savior. Everything in the Bible points to Jesus. And even though His grace is sufficient to cover all our sins, we have to remember that other people are watching us, seeing how we act and what we do.

We have to realize that more than just going to God all the time when we make mistakes, we have to earnestly seek forgiveness and then repent, turn away from "the sins that so easily beset us." Then not only are we walking in the grace of God but we are modeling to others how much our Savior loves us. He loves us not only by forgiving us for our sins, but also by fostering changes in our lives that demonstrate that love and mercy on the outside for the rest of the world to see!

*****

Now it's your turn...

- Did you see yourself in any part of this chapter?

- Do you feel God tugging on your heart about anything? Take a few minutes to let God speak to you about areas where you could use some grace.

- What steps will you take to make your relationship with Jesus stronger?

- Do you take time to enjoy a day of rest (your own Sabbath)?

Quiet Reflections

TRUTH #3

God Wants to Place Your Feet on Solid Ground

> Before I was afflicted, I went astray; but
> now I have kept thy word...
> It is good for me that I have been afflicted;
> that I might learn thy statues.
> —Psalm 119:67, 119:71

Have you ever felt like your life was in total chaos, spinning out of control, spinning you around in every direction? And then just about the time you feel like you have a foothold, your foot slips, and you fall back into the abyss of the chaos around you. If you have ever felt this way, or if you find yourself feeling this way now, I'm here to tell you, you're not alone. And it doesn't mean that you don't believe in God, and it doesn't mean that you don't love God. And it certainly doesn't mean that God doesn't love you or has forgotten you.

In fact, just the opposite is true. Part of the reason that your life may be in chaos and that you feel like it's spiraling out of control could be that you have lost your beacon. The good news is that God is always there calling out to you through any storm, beckoning you to turn your eyes back to Him. In some cases, it may be God calling you to come to Him for the first time in your life. I know this because I've lived it.

There was a time not so long ago when I thought I had my life all lined out. In fact, I was the one whom the pastor's wife said she never worried about falling. I mentioned that in a previous chapter, but what I want to talk about now is my life after the fall, my life in the midst of the storm, and the hurricane I call the next three years.

I thought I had it all figured out. I had finally gotten the job that I wanted. I was in the relationship I thought I had always wanted. I had moved to a new, larger city away from the country, away from my past. I was making more money than I had ever made in my life. I thought I had it all under control. But that's when the chaos started. I began to realize that all the decisions that I had made over the previous year had created this hurricane or tsunami or tornado or whatever you want to call it.

Regardless of the term, my life had spun completely out of control. I felt like I was a puppet. Like I was no longer making any of the decisions about my life. Those decisions were being made for me, and I had no control over what was happening, or at least it seemed that way. I was losing everything, including my mind. And I didn't know what to do or how to stop the storm around me.

It got so bad that I finally ended up in the hospital due to what they thought was cardiac arrest. The cardiologist soon discovered that my heart itself, the muscle, was just fine. The problem was the immense amount of stress that I was putting on my heart both physically and emotionally as I was trying my best to just get my feet grounded in the storm I was in. I lost focus of everything going on around me and sometimes I wanted it all to just be over. It was the most bizarre feeling to realize that my life was such a mess, barely recognizable, and I didn't know how to stop the storm around me or how to put my feet back on solid ground.

I prayed, I sought God, but I found myself alone in a storm, bewildered, suicidal even. If something didn't change, whether it be by taking my life or my life being taken, things were going to come to an end pretty soon. And that shook me to my core.

One of the things that the cardiologist recommended was that I get counseling or therapy. I left it off for a long time. After all, I was a psychology major. Why would I need counseling.? I already knew all about it. But did I? Or was I in such a storm that I couldn't even see how to get out of it? The answer was obvious. I needed help! Enter a heavenly angel named Valerie.

Valerie was the therapist assigned to me after my initial consultation at a therapy session. I had broken down and just left it all on the floor. The intake officer listened to everything I had to say, took notes, and then gave me to this woman for help. Of course, I was pessimistic at first. I didn't want to pour my heart out to someone else and be judged. I knew the things I had done were wrong, and I knew that there was really nothing I could do about any of it. I had sacrificed too much. The cost was too great. There was no fixing the mess I was in. And I didn't need some person with a psychology or counseling degree to tell me all of that. I already knew my life was screwed up. What was she going to do to help me anyway? But God knew exactly what I needed in that moment.

Because, you see, they could've put me with anybody. I have heard stories of therapy sessions. I have seen the way that "they" handle people, trying to scientifically pick their brains and talk to them about their psyche. That wasn't going to help me. In His infinite wisdom, God knew exactly what I needed because He knew what was wrong.

He moved in a miraculous way and set me up with the only counselor in my opinion who could've helped me through my storm. Here I sat in front of a complete stranger pouring out my deepest and most painful thoughts and memories, and she just sat there and listened. She didn't nod and smile, or jot down notes, or do any of the things I was expecting. She just sat there and listened.

After what seemed like hours of me gushing out all the pent-up frustrations and pain I had been harboring on my own, Valerie asked if she could draw me a picture. She simply drew two images. When she showed them to me, it changed my life forever, so much so that years later I can still see the images she drew clearly.

The first was a chair with me sitting in it with a cross at my feet. Surrounding me were arrows going all different directions (representing chaos). The other image was of a chair with the cross sitting in it and me at the foot of the chair, and all the arrows were pointing out in a circular pattern surrounding me and the chair (representing peace). Looking back now, the arrows kind of resembled a shield around me.

Valerie helped me to see that the reason my life was in chaos was because I had taken Christ off the throne of my heart. Somewhere along the way, I had started focusing more on what I wanted than what God wanted for me. When you put yourself on the throne of your life, bad things happen. Once I could see the problem, I finally knew what I needed to do to get the chaos of my life back in balance. I had to put God back on the throne of my life! But it wasn't just about asking for forgiveness. I had done that over and over again. It was more than that. I had to trust Him to guide me out of the chaos.

I had to start believing that I really was forgiven and start forgiving myself. Through further therapy sessions with this angel from God, the healing began. When I started owning the mistakes I had made and began to believe that I had been forgiven, I found the strength to finally move forward with my life.

Now there was no going back. It took several years to finally get to a place where I could accept that I could never undo what I had done. The damage was permanent, but the pain didn't have to be. I could move forward. And I could trust God to turn my ashes back into something beautiful. I just had to be willing to let Him do it. And that's the part I wanted to get to. That's the thing that I wanted you to know.

You see, no matter how crazy your life has gotten, no matter what you've done wrong, no matter what mistakes or choices you've made that have led you to this place where you're at now, I'm here to tell you, God is bigger than your storm. God *will* move. God *will* put your life back together again. It may not be the same life you had, and truthfully it probably shouldn't be, but He *will* turn your ashes into beauty if you let Him.

But you've got to give it to Him…all of it! You've got to throw your hands up, and you've got to say, "I surrender," and you've got to give it to Him. And then, you've got to put one foot in front of the other, and you've got to start walking forward, trusting Him to lead you out of your storm and back into a world that makes sense again. He did it for me. He will do it for you. He loves you that much.

> To appoint unto them that mourn in Zion, to give unto them beauty for ashes, the oil of joy for mourning, the garment of praise for the spirit of heaviness; that they might be called trees of righteousness, the planting of the LORD, that he might be glorified. (Isaiah 61:3)

*****

Now it's your turn:

- Are you in a storm?

- Do you believe God wants to lead you out of that storm?

- What are you holding back? Give it to Him!

- What is God speaking to your heart to do now?

Quiet Reflections

TRUTH #4

The Blessings of God Are Real

> Now the God of hope fill you with
> all joy and peace in believing,
> that ye may abound in hope, through
> the power of the Holy Ghost.
>
> —Romans 15:13

I still remember that moment like it was yesterday. We were struggling financially, camped out in that stretch of time between June and September, edging toward August, when my summer teacher money was about to run out. We had had some unexpected financial blows, and the extra work I had planned to do to rally our finances was blocked by a family death followed by my mom's back injury. But somehow, I had held on to four hundred dollars in the bank and three hundred dollars in cash, enough to make the truck payment and skimp on groceries until my husband got paid, and then maybe, just maybe, we could skimp some more and make it until I got paid in September. I knew I had some anxiety, but I thought I was managing it well enough. I had faith God was going to carry us through… somehow. He always did.

I had just settled into bed that night, convincing myself there was nothing to worry about, that we would be okay. Then at midnight that all changed in an instant. I heard the familiar ding of my phone signaling that I had gotten a text message. Who on earth would text me at midnight? And then it hit me, and my heart skipped a beat. Was it the bank? Had I somehow forgotten a payment that was auto deducted, something to put me below my arbitrary seventy-five dollars remaining balance mark? I searched my mind and held my breath, reassuring myself that I still had three hundred dollars cash in my drawer, something I had kept back to help pay the September rent. I could pull a little from that if needed.

So with a deep breath, I reached over and picked up my phone...and then panic ensued. I wasn't down to seventy-five dollars. I was negative three hundred twenty dollars! Wait...*what?* How? Why? Oh my god. What now? I forced myself to log into my bank account online to see what had happened. That's when I realized that, unexpectedly, a car payment for over seven hundred dollars had been deducted from my account. And it was midnight. And there was nothing I could do in that moment. *Nothing*.

I tried to pray. I tried telling myself out loud that it would be okay, that it wasn't as bad as it looked. Despite my best efforts, I began tossing and turning, my mind unable to shut off as I quickly ran numbers back and forth, back and forth, back and forth again. There was simply no way to make it now! I could feel the panic rising higher and higher, my pulse racing, my heart and head pounding. It was getting hard to breathe. Every possible negative outcome came flooding through my mind, a continuous mental assault on my sense of calm. *Enough.* I practically yelled it. *Enough!*

It was then that I jumped out of bed, headed to my prayer closet, pushed the door closed so the dogs couldn't get in, and threw myself down not just on my knees but face almost to the ground in a kneeling position, crying out to God in my anguish, begging for peace to wash over me, for a promise, for a reassurance that "this too shall pass." For close to ten minutes I stayed there, pouring my heart out to God. I was broken, my faith sucked away as a black hole of fear and doubt tried to envelop me. I had been so careful to work every angle, borrowed from Peter to pay Paul, as my mom always used to say. I had stretched us to the limit, and then some. Our only shot was that money. And now it was all gone...every penny, and it was only July 18th.

And then…God. Just as quickly as the fear had set in before, peace began filling my heart, my mind, and finally my body. I began to breathe normally. My mind became clear. I would put the three hundred dollars I had in cash, along with another twenty dollars I had in my car, into my bank account the next morning so I wouldn't incur any service charges, and then I would do the only thing I knew to do…let go and let God.

I think I was asleep before my bedsheets even got warm. And I slept all night long. Praise God! But that's not the end of the story. His peace, His wonderful peace, didn't just get me through the night. It carried me (us) all the way through to my September payday. And it continues to carry me. God's peace that passes all understanding…I get that now. I didn't understand how I would get through, but God's peace passed by all my worries and fears. And I still can't explain how we made it, but we did.

If I tried to sit down and map it all out on paper, the numbers simply wouldn't add up. It was an impossible situation. But impossible situations are God's specialty. The only explanation I can give is that God gave us favor. God gave us protection. He rebuked the devourer. He parted the mighty Jordan and carried us safely across to dry land. And now when I sing songs of worship about His peace and His protection, I can't stop myself from raising my hands to heaven and singing with all my might! And that is all I need. Amen.

> Even in the darkest valley,
> Your peace is rushing through me.
> Even with the fire surrounding,
> I know that You stand with me.
> Even as the flames rise higher,
> I'm safe, I will not fear.
> I can hear Your voice like thunder.
> My Hope and my Deliverer.
> (Red Rock Worship)

That was September. At the time of writing, it is now Christmas Eve. I thought this chapter was finished. But as I tuned in to the

Spirit's leading, God told me to work on "Chapter 11" some more. That was the working title of this chapter at the time of writing. I wasn't even sure what the chapter contained until I logged in and scrolled down to it. "The blessings of God are real." That's the title. And it's also a mighty truth! I could sit and ponder literally all day on all the blessings in and throughout my life: my husband, my three beautiful and kind-hearted daughters, a good job, an amazing church family, friends…

Friends. God stopped me right there. It wasn't too long ago that I was having a pity party over not having any *real* friends. You know, the kind that would go the extra mile for you, be there when you most needed them? I just didn't think I really had any anymore. Oh sure, I have my husband, my best friend. And I have work acquaintances. But we don't ever really hang out. If I found myself going through something, a true crisis, would anyone come to my aid?

Well, God answered that question about three weeks ago (as of the time of this writing). You see, I had gotten sick—*really* sick! Like, thought I might could actually die from it sick. And then my husband, who was caring for me, got sick, too! That's when God revealed to me just how blessed I really am. So many people poured into us and our situation. Some brought food, some sent gift cards for food deliveries, many texted, prayed, or called. Some helped with lesson plans for my classroom. Many expressed concerns and sent well wishes. And it was a wonderful reminder that I do have friends.

But there was one friend who reminded me that He had been there all along, the "friend that sticketh closer than a brother." When I found myself physically unable to manage the constant coughing anymore, when I couldn't seem to get any air in my desperate lungs, when I hit the point where I realized I had waited too long to go to the ER, that's when my *best* friend surrounded me with His presence. I'm talking about Jesus.

I had just gotten off the phone with my pastor, who had called to see what he could do for me, and I was coughing so hard I couldn't even speak. As we said goodbye, he promised that he and his wife would pray for me as soon as he hung up. I tried to get to the kitchen to find something, anything, to get air into my lungs, when I finally collapsed (nearly fainted) onto my knees with my head buried in the seat of my rocking chair, crying out to God, first in my mind, and then eventually, as I fought for breath, my voice…*JESUS, HELP ME! I can't breathe!*

I can't explain it any other way than this. As I humbly postured on my knees, head buried in my chair, I began to feel the presence of Jesus surrounding me. I began inhaling His presence, one deep refreshing breath at a time as the Holy Spirit opened my lungs and throat, making way for air, for oxygen, for relief. I lay there for I can't tell you how long, just breathing in Jesus and life.

And as I did, God began speaking to me, reminding me of how precious life is, how short our time on this earth is, how much I still had left to do for the kingdom, how I needed to get back to working on this book, and how loved I am by our Savior! And that is when I was reminded how blessed I am, how blessed all of us are as children of the Most High. In that moment, I suddenly remembered just how true it is. The blessings of God are real!

May God show you just how blessed you are today and every day. He is our Creator. He is our Savior. He is our Redeemer. He is our Comforter. And He is our friend. Praise God Almighty, His blessings are real!

*****

I have no questions for you to ponder this time, only a request. Reflect on your own life, all the times God has brought you through something that seemed impossible. Now begin to praise Him for all the blessings in your life. Record your thoughts on the next page. When you finish, I hope you will keep reading. I have more truths to share with you!

Quiet Reflections

TRUTH #5

He Will Never Leave You or Forsake You

> Be strong and of a good courage,
> fear not, nor be afraid of them:
> for the LORD thy God, he it is that doth go with thee;
> he will not fail thee, nor forsake thee.
> —Deuteronomy 31:6

I've been through some pretty rough times in my life, mostly due to my own foolish choices, but not always. Some things came at me with little to no warning, and I just had to weather the storm until it was over. But one thing I have found to always be true: God never left me.

In the Bible, the Lord promises us that He will never leave us or forsake us. To leave would mean to go away from us, and to forsake would mean to turn His back on us when we need Him. Once you accept Jesus into your heart, He comes and resides within you. His Spirit inhabits your soul. You can feel Him there, hear Him speaking to you as He provides you with wisdom and guidance. It's the beautiful, unexplainable peace you feel at the altar when you worship, or in those moments when you know you did something God wanted you to do, some unselfish act out of obedience, when He pours out a special blessing on you.

But that feeling isn't always there (though it could be). Sometimes, we yearn to feel His presence, hear Him speak a Word to us, but we feel abandoned, and He appears to be silent. That is when the enemy tries to convince us that we are alone. But the truth is, we are *never* alone. God is *always* there, watching over us and speaking to us, guiding us even in those lonely, quiet moments. The problem is that we just haven't learned to fine-tune our spiritual ears to listen. Or we have purposely chosen to turn a deaf ear so we can't hear what His Spirit is speaking to us.

Today was a prime example. I woke up at 7:00 a.m. with a song repeating in my mind. I listened to the words for a few minutes, decided to lie back down and ponder it, and fell back asleep. I woke up again around 8:00 a.m. with that same song in my head. Now I had a choice. I could brush it off and go on with my day (turn the TV on, get lost in the land of social media, work on my grad school lesson for the week, etc.). But I decided instead to pay attention to what I was hearing. These were the words that were going through my head:

> So I'll breathe it in. My soul needs oxygen.
> Without You I'm incomplete.
> Something in the air, in the atmosphere.
> You're pullin' me like gravity.
> Gotta be still and breathe…
> I know Your Word is worth my attention.
> But I lose Your voice
> when I stand at a distance.
> I wanna feel Your heartbeat
> move with the rhythm.
> How can I when I won't shut up and listen?
> When distractions drive me to the edge,
> You say, "Come to Me and you'll find rest."
> (Colton Dixon, "Breathe")

So that's the song that was running in circles through my head this morning. Nothing else. Just that. And that's one of the many ways that God speaks to us. He speaks to us in song lyrics we wake up to, in scriptures that are suddenly recalled to mind, and sometimes just flat-out audibly, telling us what He wants us to do, and reassuring us that we are never alone. When I can't hear Him and I really need Him to speak to me, I've learned that I am still learning how to listen.

So what do you do when you get to one of those storms in life when you feel like you are all alone and God is not there with you? Well, first, as the song says, "Shut up and listen!" And actually, the Bible says to "be still and know that I am God." Always try that first. It's a good starting point, and half the time, it's all you need to do to hear what God is saying to you.

But what if that doesn't work? That's when you go to the Word. Open your Bible to the first book that comes to mind and start reading. I can't tell you how many times I have done this and found exactly the advice or bit of wisdom I needed to hear for my circumstances. If you don't have a Bible handy, try playing the first Christian song on your media player that comes to mind, and look up the lyrics, so you really *see* them.

If neither of those things work, trying good old-fashioned getting down on your knees and crying out to God. I don't mean sitting down and reciting a three-point prayer that you've memorized or said a hundred times. I mean just find a space where you can be alone and cry out to Jesus, and then be still and listen. You might be surprised just how quickly He will answer you. I'm still amazed sometimes when He answers so audibly.

Now, I have to be honest here and tell you there is a chance that you will have times in your life where no matter what you try to do, you might not hear God. It's happened to me a few times along the way. Sometimes, for whatever reason, you can just feel alienated and alone. That's when you have to pray for God to shed light on what is keeping you from hearing Him.

You see, I told you He never leaves us, but that doesn't mean that we don't wander away from Him sometimes. Sin, rebellion, disobedience, laziness, lack of effort, not studying the Word, not lifting your voice in praise and worship, pretty much putting God on a shelf in your closet, taking Him out only when it's convenient for you… any of those things can draw you away from feeling God's presence and hearing His voice.

If I never talk to a friend of mine, never call, never text, never comment or "like" something on social media, and then out of the blue decide I really need to talk to her and call her on the phone, chances are, unless she's feeling the same way, she probably won't take the time to answer, and will let it just go to voice mail to check later.

I think we've all probably done that at some point, prioritizing if we have time to talk to someone we haven't spoken to in a long time, wondering what they want, deciding to screen the call to see what they want before we return the call. What about that friend who only calls you when they need you to do something for them? Yeah, you know the one. How many times have we all let *that* go to voice mail? I'm not judging. I'm just as guilty, and I'm working on it.

Now, think about God for a few minutes. He is God, He is all-knowing and all-seeing. We established that in an earlier chapter. He knows our needs before we ever ask. But He also created us to have a relationship with Him. A real one, where we talk to Him and share our world with Him. So what happens when we go days or even weeks at a time without talking to Him? Thankfully, He doesn't screen our calls! But we may still need to do some soul-searching to find our way back to feeling His presence.

> For I know the thoughts that I think toward you, saith the Lord, thoughts of peace, and not of evil, to give you an expected end. (Jeremiah 29:11)

I have to remind myself daily that He is God and I am not. I uncovered a journal this morning while I was putting something else away. I can't exactly remember when I wrote in the journal as I didn't date the entries, but it's been within the last year or so. As I was thumbing through the pages, I came across a list that I wrote and entitled "Painful Experiences."

It's a list of thirty things that I have gone through in my life that were painful. Some of those items include my parents separating, my mom abandoning me in South Dakota and coming back to Arkansas when I was ten, being a single parent on welfare in my twenties and being suicidal, being pregnant alone, my dad dying, the trials I went through as a high school principal, watching my own daughter hurt so deeply over the issues with her son, and then seeing her lose her faith…I could go on and on. And I could add a few more things to that list! But that's not the point of the chapter.

At the end of my list, I wrote several things. First of all was the quote from Jeremiah 29:11. I also wrote, "The God who did it before can do it again." I wrote, "The God who got me here will get me there." I wrote, "God is working His good, pleasing, and perfect plan for my life in a thousand ways I am not even aware of. Everything in my past is in preparation for something in my future." And finally, "Even when I have a setback, God has already prepared my comeback!"

That last one is a pretty profound thought. Even in the midst of my turmoil when I feel like my world is going backward, God is already in my future preparing my comeback, but not just a "comeback," a moving forward, getting better, getting stronger and wiser and more Christlike.

You see, it would've been easy during any one of those times on my list to quit, to give up and stay right where I was. Or, even worse, to do something drastic that couldn't be undone, like taking my own life, which I did consider on a few occasions, but thankfully not anymore. You see, I realize looking back that God has *always* been there. He wasn't the one causing my pain. My own choices and mistakes led me into most of the circumstances on that list. Granted not all of them were my doing, but regardless, God was always there.

He was the whisper to my heart that told me things were going to be okay. He was in the unexpected phone call from a friend I hadn't heard from in years saying that I was on their heart. He was in the email out of the blue from someone with a scripture that I needed to hear just at that moment. He was in the song playing on the radio when I started my car. He was the urge to open the Word and read of His promises and His love for me. And sometimes, He was the audible voice that told me exactly what I needed to hear or do or think or say to get me out of the situation that I was in.

He was and has always been the thing that has kept me going. He *is* the one that keeps me going. My God, my Savior, my protector, my friend. Even in my darkest hour when I felt like I had no hope, God was right there beside me, speaking to my heart, surrounding me with His love. I didn't always know it, but still He was there. His Word promises that He will never leave us or forsake us. Even in the midst of our greatest storms in life, God is on our side, fighting battles for us that we can't even begin to realize or understand. And for that, I am grateful.

He is the breath that I breathe. He is the reason I am still alive. He is the reason I never gave up, never quit, never completely lost hope. He is my everything. Even when I didn't know it, He was there. He always has been, and He always will be. He loves me that much.

And He loves you that much, too! Look around you at the beauty that exists in the wind on a hot summer day, the trees going from green to yellow to brown to green again, the sun in the sky during the day and stars in the heavens at night, the rainbows after a storm, the sheer glory of a newborn's face, the cuddly adorableness of kittens and puppies, the breath of life itself…all beautiful, and all reminders of His love for us. Our God created all of that for us. And that same God created you and me, breathed life into us from the moment we were conceived, and He continues to breathe life into us, sometimes quite literally.

So how can anyone ever truly be alone or without hope? God loves us so much He was willing to lay down His life for us! A God like that would *never* leave us alone to fight our way through the storms of life. He's there…even when we can't see Him or feel Him…He's there!

*****

So, again, no questions for you this time. Just a request. Close your eyes, get quiet, and listen…breathe in, breathe out, hear the beating of your heart, feel the space around you, and maybe, just maybe, you will hear Him speaking to you right now! Give it a try. But don't forget to listen. If you do hear Him speak, write down what He says so you'll remember it!

Quiet Reflections

TRUTH #6

He Never Fails Us

"You've never failed me."

How many people do you know who can say that about someone else? I'd love to say there are people in my life who have never failed me. I'd also like to say there are people in my life whom I have never failed. Both would be miserable untruths. The truth is people are human. We all make mistakes. We might be really good in some moments, but then fail in others. I have already mentioned my former pastor's wife telling me that she never worried about me because I had a strong foundation. Imagine her disbelief and how much it hurt her (and the church) when one of the "strongest believers" didn't just fail but had fallen headlong into sin.

It happens. Sin will creep into your thought life, and if left unchecked, before you know it, it will boldly declare itself in your physical life as well. But that isn't what this chapter is about. If you want to know about failing and falling, you can go back to the first eight or so chapters of this book and you will find as many examples of a failed life as you want.

The simple truth is that I failed myself and my family and, most importantly, I failed God. But the bigger truth, the focal point of this chapter, is that despite all my failures, one thing remained true. God has *never* failed *me*! Not when I was high on the mountain and not when I found myself in danger of the pits of hell. God has always been there for me, in the right way, at the right place, and always at the right time. When I look back on my life and think about all the places I have been and all the things I have done, no matter what the circumstance, whether I dug my own hole or someone pushed me in, God was *always* there to save me, to pick me up, dust me off, and set my feet back on solid ground.

You see, the devil would have us believe that we can never live up to the life we are called to live, and in a way that is true. But the flip side of that is that God never asked us to. God doesn't require us to be perfect. "For all have sinned and fallen short..." Even Adam and Eve made mistakes—a big one, in fact. Yet God didn't abandon them. Peter denied even knowing Christ (after walking with Him), yet Jesus forgave him and inspired him to write a good portion of the New Testament. David had an affair and then had the woman's husband killed to try to hide it, yet King David was later remembered as "a man after God's own heart."

You see, that is the kind of God we serve. This wondrous Creator of heaven and earth, who spoke life into existence, the Alpha and the Omega, the beginning and the end, the El-Shaddai, the Lord of lords, the King of kings, the great I Am...yes, *that* God has never failed to be everything I need, everything I could *ever* need.

And the miracle is that despite all my failures in life, He still watches over me. And no matter what you've done in your life, whatever messes you have made, He still watches over you, too. Jesus said He would never leave us or forsake us. Not even death itself can separate us from the love of God. Paul, the famous persecutor of Christians, who later had a life-changing encounter with Jesus on the road to Damascus, penned the following.

> For I am persuaded, that neither death, nor life, nor angels, nor principalities, nor powers, nor things present, nor things to come, nor heights, nor depths, nor any other creature, shall be able to separate us from the love of God, which is in Christ Jesus our Lord. (Romans 8:38–39)

Let that sink in. God never fails us, not in death, or life, in the past, in the present, in the future, on the mountains, in the valleys, through persecution and trials, mistakes, missteps, all-out failure… *nothing* can get in the way of God's love for us. He loves us that much!

*****

Think about your own mistakes in life, the places you have gone, the choices you have made, and the things you've had to go through. Can you look back over your life and see how God has taken care of you? How He has brought you out of some things? How He still wants to bring you out of some things? What would your life look like if He hadn't? Ponder that for a moment, and then record your thoughts in the space provided.

Quiet Reflections

Truth #7

You Can Do All Things through Christ

An excerpt from my journal, dated July 9, 2017…

When my husband drinks I can't handle being around him. I still love him and want to watch over him and keep him safe, but I can't be intimate. The behavior keeps me away. I want to be able to spend quality time with him but his behavior when he drinks keeps that from happening. And I can't stop him or make him stop. He has to do it. He has to be the one to either turn away from the drinking or ask me for help. All I can do is watch over him, keep a distance, and let him know I don't approve and that it's keeping him from me. God is much the same way when we are sinning, choosing to put something else between us and Him. He's still there watching over us and keeping us from severe hurt, and He's waiting for us to put away the sin and come back to Him so we can spend time with Him in fellowship and intimacy. But in the middle of the sin, though He appears to be far away He is still there watching over us and waiting. He said He would never leave us or forsake us. In the same way, as much as I hate the behavior, I still love the man. And if I am to love him like Christ loves him, I won't leave him or forsake him either, though I also won't stop him if he chooses to walk away from me. I'll be right here waiting for the prodigal to return.

Let me just stop and tell you how good God is! I'm writing this chapter less than two years after I recorded that entry, and let me tell you, *wow*! Just wow, God! I don't want to get into the details of my husband's journey. That's his story to tell. But I will tell you from my perspective. I stayed put. I dug deep. I prayed, I cried, I anointed the doorways with oil (several times), I threw myself at the altar, repeatedly asking God to do a work in my husband's life because I knew underneath all the pain of his tortured past, there was a beautiful soul and a powerful testimony waiting to escape. I don't know how. I don't know exactly when, but God got ahold of my husband and, before I knew it, not only did he rededicate his life to Jesus, but he got baptized as well!

And guess what? The drinking *stopped*! Hallelujah, praise God! I thank God every day for the wondrous work He did in our home, in our marriage, in our family, and in what He's continuing to do in my husband's life. I still don't think I am giving God enough credit for everything that has happened since that miracle. We have grown as a couple; we have both grown stronger in our faith, and now, my favorite moments are when I walk in the room and see him deep in his thoughts as he reads the Word of God. It is now that I finally understand why God repeatedly told me to "love him like I love you." I am married to the man of my dreams, my heart's desire, and it is all to God's glory!

There is so much more I want to share, but that's his story to tell. All I can say is this: All things *do* work together for our *good* through Christ who gives us strength! Hallelujah and amen!

> Nay, in all these things we are more than conquerors through him that loved us. (Romans 8:37)

> I can do all things through Christ which strengtheneth me. (Philippians 4:13)

*****

I got my miracle. What miracle do you need in your own life? Maybe alcohol isn't something you or your spouse struggle with. Maybe it's something else. Do you believe God can change things around? Do you believe that He really does work all things together for our good? Spend some time in prayer, asking God to help you with the burdens of your heart. Then when you get your miracle, come back and write it down so it can encourage you when you need your next miracle.

Quiet Reflections

TRUTH #8

We Are All Missionaries

Everywhere you look, there's a screen. In our hands, on the wall, every room, every place we go. And what's on it is purposely prepared to capture and keep our attention for as long as possible, distracting us from the reality and the people around us, feeding us what someone else wants us to see, think, and feel.

> Let the words of my mouth, and the meditation of my heart, be acceptable in thy sight, O Lord, my strength, and my redeemer. (Psalms 19:14)

Unless what's on the screen or playing in our ears is the Word, we are continuously inundating our minds (and our spirit) with worldly desires and pleasures. I'm not against watching a little TV (I personally love *MasterChef*), but how do we know when it's too much, especially when it's too much of the wrong thing? Have you ever gone to the gym and tried *not* looking at the TVs? I have to literally close my eyes or, next thing I know, I'm more focused on what's on that rectangular screen than what I'm doing to my body. Even if I've got worship music playing, I still catch myself zoning out of what's in my ear and focusing on what's in my eyes.

More than just that, what I notice I'm not doing is looking around. I'm not paying any attention to what's going on around me or who's around me. When I go to the gym, that's often by design. I like to tune everyone else out and just do my own thing. At a restaurant, if I'm eating alone, I guarantee you I'm on my phone, again tuning out the world. Seems harmless enough, right? *You don't mess with me, and I won't mess with you.* Everyone just minding their own business and going on with their life...

> Neither do men light a candle, and put it under a bushel, but on a candlestick; and it giveth light unto all that are in the house. (Matthew 5:15)

Here I am walking around with the light of Jesus, the key to not only eternal salvation but hope and courage for the trials of this current life, and what do I do with my candle? I put it under a bushel and just go on about my day, potentially tuning out people around me who desperately need to see the light of Jesus. So how do I get out of my bubble and start sharing the good news about our Savior?

I once had the pleasure of meeting a special woman, the wife of an evangelist. Her greatest legacy, according to all who know her, is that everywhere she goes, no matter who she meets, within minutes, they know she loves Jesus. It's in her smile, it's in her voice, and it's in everything she says. Her candle is so bright that darkness has no choice but to run and hide. When I think about how I go into my own little world at the gym, I can tell you that my candle is not shining as brightly as it could be, especially if I'm ignoring my surroundings. I'm still working on that, even as I pen the last chapters.

> Go ye therefore, and teach all nations, baptizing them in the name of the Father, and of the Son, and of the Holy Ghost: Teaching them to observe all things whatsoever I have commanded you: and, lo, I am with you always, even unto the end of the world. (Matthew 28:19–20)

Everywhere we go, we are called by Jesus to be missionaries. One of the biggest things I worry about when I get to heaven is to find out that I missed the opportunity to win someone over to Christ before it was too late. So even though I'm not as great with my personal encounters as the woman I mentioned, I can't afford to tune people out either. Not even at the gym!

So, for me it starts with this book. It starts by having the courage to record the mess I've made of my life and how Jesus, through His unlimited grace, has picked me up out of the miry clay, set my feet on solid ground, and is doing a work in me. It continues with finding the courage to let it be published, for my life to become transparent and real to others. It continues further with each person who picks up this book and begins reading about the amazing blessings of God and how the devil tries to rob us of those blessings. And, hopefully, it will continue to spread, as one person shares this book with another person, and they share it with another, and so on… And before we know it, this "little light of mine" is going to be shining brightly as a beacon in the darkness, not for my glory but for His! That's the legacy I want to leave.

Quiet Reflections

The Conclusion of the Matter

Give Me Oil in My Lamp

Keep me burning! They say a watched pot will never boil, but when it comes to faith, the opposite is true. You have to continuously attend to your faith to keep it on fire.

I've had a fire inside since I was fourteen. Possibly even before then, as I certainly believe in predestination. Predestination doesn't mean only certain people are picked out to be saved, rather that God already knows who He will be able to use and who will be unfruitful, unprofitable, lukewarm…

But it's a mistake to believe that once you are saved you will naturally stay on fire for God. Good ground (remember the parable) doesn't just naturally produce brilliant vegetation on its own. Yes, it will grow things, but what grows depends on what is planted, and whether the weeds are pulled regularly. Otherwise they will take over that good ground, overtake the good vegetation, and, soon, if left unattended, you will have a weed garden.

For example, I have good ground in my backyard. I can grow awesome bell peppers and okra, tomatoes and squash, corn, just about anything that will grow in the south. But I can also grow weeds and lots of them, and much more quickly than the desired vegetation. I have learned a great deal about growing vegetables over the last several years.

1. You have to prep the ground before planting.
2. You have to give time and space to your harvest.
3. You must water it daily.
4. You have to weed it regularly.
5. The more you tend to it, the larger and more beautiful your harvest will become.
6. Left unattended, your crops will begin to shrink, and your weeds will choke out their life, and the outside predators will begin attacking, unless you have it properly shielded.

I was fervent about my garden in the beginning. Then I got tired of working so hard, took my harvest for granted, and let it grow on its own. The results are that I lost a great deal of the potential harvest, weeds began taking over, and all that was left was some tough okra and baby peppers. And those are dead now, too. So what happened? I mean, I wanted to garden. I put in the time and effort to start my garden; I watered it for a while. But then what? I got lukewarm!

So how does gardening apply to faith? When I got saved at fourteen, I was hungry. I began investing the time and effort to grow my faith garden. I read the Word daily, I memorized scripture, I got on my knees at night and sincerely reached out to God, I attended church every time the door was open, and I was on fire! It gave me a natural desire to be bold—to witness to people, to read my Bible in public, to go knocking on doors, etc. I was tending my faith garden, and prepping for a harvest for my Master.

But when weeds started growing, I didn't take the time to pull them. I mowed them down a time or two, but I left the roots intact. Before I knew it, just two years later, my once beautiful walk with God was in jeopardy of being overrun by weeds, and my fire was being choked out of existence.

This is the place where I say I'm glad I used to keep a journal. Without those writings, I would've forgotten two important things.

First, it's my fault I let my garden grow up with weeds. Second, God was always there, reminding me I had a garden, asking me to come back and tend it again because it still has the ability to be good ground. But I was stubborn, and it took a lot of tribulation in my life for me to realize how much I needed that garden and my Savior. But that's another chapter.

What I learned about being lukewarm is that it leads to pain and, eventually, death. A garden left unattended will eventually die, one way or another. The other thing I learned is the more that you tend your garden, the stronger your faith will grow, and the larger the harvest will be when you are finished. More than anything, I want my Savior to say, "Good job, well done. Welcome home." In order to do that, I've got to keep my fire burning, avoid being lukewarm, and do everything I can for the kingdom in the meantime.

As I finish the final edit of this book, I want to make one final plea to those who may still be sitting on the fence with their faith. It's a Sunday. The pastor of our church just started a new series today on the End Times. As I was worshipping toward the end of the service, the Lord impressed upon me two very strong visions. The first is that, as Christians, we don't have as much time left as we think we do. Jesus is returning soon, and it will happen so fast, faster than you can blink your eyes! *Blink*! The church will be gone.

The second is a warning for those who are lukewarm or just playing games, who are banking on possibly getting things right after the Rapture and still making it to heaven. Total chaos is going to happen when people disappear in the blink of an eye. Cars are going to crash, trains are going to derail, and planes are going to fall from the sky as their pilots and drivers are taken. Those resulting crashes are going to take lives, and then the ensuing confusion, riots, and violence as wars break out all over are going to take more lives.

The devil will focus his attention on wiping out as many potential new believers as possible. You aren't guaranteed the time to change your mind, repent, and get things right. After the trumpet sounds and the dead in Christ rise and those believers left on earth are taken, you aren't guaranteed another second of your life. Please hear my heart! Please don't wait. Fall on your knees and beg God for forgiveness and put your faith and hope in him. It's not about trying to be perfect. It's about believing in the only name that can save you, and His name is Jesus! I want all my family and friends in eternity with me. Please don't miss the trumpet's call. Take care of your eternity right now. And then keep your lamp full of oil until Jesus returns!

Epilogue

Your Greatest Enemy Is Fear

Fear isn't real. It only appears to be real. But real or not, it can stop you in your tracks. It's the thoughts that grip you in the middle of the night. It's the trembling of your heart and your mind as you feel your life spiraling out of control. Your heart pounds in anticipation of what you can only imagine will be the worst possible outcome. For something you can't see, taste, or touch, it sure can cause a lot of anxiety. And, left unchecked, it can leave you cowering in the corner. Or…it can drive you to your knees. What happens next totally depends on what you chose to do.

Fear: false evidence appearing real.

It's that phone call that keeps coming, the one you're afraid to answer because you know it's yet another bill collector demanding money. It's that email from your boss asking you when you can come for a meeting in the office. It's not wanting to check your bank account balance because you know you don't have any money left. It's the sinking feeling in the pit of your stomach as yet another appliance goes out or your car breaks down just when the warranty has expired. It's wondering why your spouse isn't home on time, maybe due to an accident or something worse.

All these thoughts and feelings have one thing in common. They take the unknown and turn it into the worst possible outcome, even before you know (I mean really know) what your options are. And fear is something I have known many times my life. But the one thing I have come to know is that in the face of fear, in the unrelenting anxiety of the impossible, God stands strong, conquering the flesh and replacing fear with peace, peace that even the impossible is possible with God.

Fear doesn't want you to know that God is bigger. Fear doesn't want you to believe that the same God who rescued the Israelites from Pharaoh's army wants to rescue you. Fear is a taker, and it will take away every bit of peace and rob you of every bit of joy you have. And then fear will sit back and laugh at you as you spiral into depression, worry, pain, suicidal thoughts, addictions, and sometimes even death.

But…

Fear doesn't want you to know you have a weapon, and it's as close as your knees are to the floor when you bow your head and your heart and just say, "Jesus." Try it! Then when you find your power in God, share your own story with someone else. You just might be the light they are looking for! May God bless you all.

> You've walked in her shoes
> You've heard the lies
> You know the pain… Come alive
> He's still the truth, He's still the life
> He's still the way
> Could this be the day
> that you come to the rescue?
> (Casting Crowns, "One Awkward Moment")

About the Author

D. A. Coffer is an American writer and educator. She lives with her family in Northwest Arkansas and has been teaching and serving for over twenty years in the public school system. She gave her heart to Jesus when she was fourteen years old but ended up backsliding back into the world, spending much of her twenties running from God before finally coming to terms with her past and recommitting her life to His service. This is her first book.